These are dishes thoughtfully designed for all of life's big moments; birthday celebrations, bridal showers, and births, and the harder times, like sickness and other times of need. Sara also shares her recipes for heavy-lifting sauces that can be incorporated into multiple meals and tips for dinners that will travel well, freeze well, and feed a group.

Around Our Table embodies Sara's generous approach toward cooking, making it an indispensable resource for timeless, family-friendly meals you'll make again and again.

AROUND OUR TABLE

SPROUTED KITCHEN

AROUND
OUR TABLE

wholesome recipes to feed your
family & friends

Hardie Grant

NORTH AMERICA

for my family,
around a table with you will always be my most favorite place

"Home is wherever I'm with you"

—Edward Sharpe and the Magnetic Zeros

CONTENTS

1   Introduction

11   First Thing

53   Snacks + Starters

91   Salads + Sides

137   A Main Dish

197   Soups, Stews + Make Ahead

237   Treats

279   Dressings, Condiments + Basics

294   Menu Ideas

296   With Thanks

298   Index

Introduction

I was sitting around a table of fellow preschool moms, nursing my youngest, probably sweating, acting bright eyed, perhaps not in workout pants for once this week, but feeling completely depleted. I was in the hamster wheel of raising two young kids who I thought I could parent well while also keeping my food writing career afloat. I was the one at the table who had a reputation for healthy, beautiful food by way of my food blog, Sprouted Kitchen, and Instagram. I had fifteen years of food experience to pull from— working the sample counter at Trader Joe's, front of the house for caterers and restaurants, at a farm and bed and breakfast in Italy, as a personal chef, and finally writing my own recipes in books and online. These other moms would turn to me for dinner ideas, wondering what I was making with my one free hand, in this time of life when these little people needed so much from us. But the thing was, like the other parents, my toaster oven was full of chicken nuggets and frozen pizzas and my purse and glove compartment had granola bars and applesauce pouches for the in-between moments of these days. I loved grocery stores, but I could no longer go to three different markets in an afternoon to source my favorite ingredients or spend time online, cross-referencing the best healthy muffin recipes. In the frenzy of family life, my experience with food wasn't giving me a leg up. No one in my orbit had the mental capacity to figure out what was for dinner, me included. But I did believe it was possible. I knew how to cook well; I just needed to do it smarter. I remember coming home that day and telling my husband, Hugh, that this would be a pivot in my career. I still wanted to write and cook and share, but it would need to be less romantic and leisurely, more practical and adaptable.

Since then, my cooking has evolved to suit our current reality. I won't try to tell you that good, beautiful food happens quickly—it usually doesn't. But by planning ahead—by, say, starting a batch of granola and soup on a Sunday afternoon, making a few sauces or dressings when I have a spare ten minutes and the food processor is already out, or preparing a slaw that could be both a side dish one night and a taco topping the next—I can be halfway there when it comes to actual dinnertime. This cookbook is a collection of recipes that work for us, as well as the field notes I've collected from our meal-planning program, Sprouted Kitchen Cooking Club, an online community we created for other home cooks trying to solve these same problems.

Lately, my days are full of testing and writing and shooting recipes for the Cooking Club. Many of my hours are spent caring for our kids, taxiing Curran and Cleo to school and sports practices and playdates, squeezing in exercise, and trying to maintain some semblance of a social life myself. I am sure you have a similar juggle. Maybe you're planning to have friends over, perhaps you're wrangling children underfoot right now, maybe they're grown, or perhaps you work sixty hours a week; if you've picked up this book, my guess is you want to eat real food. You're attracted to color and fresh produce and believe that those things can be both delicious *and* nourishing. Not fussy or complicated but flavorful, casual, sometimes decadent, and beautiful food.

I frequently carry a container of my recipe samples to give to my kids' teachers or a jar full of extra soup or sauce to pass along to a friend. Sharing food is its own sort of affection. I enjoy the sourcing, the conversations, and the chaos of getting food to the table. I care about wellness and the long-term benefits of eating real food. I take care of myself and others through cooking. As my own family grows and the particulars of our life ebb and flow, I have found the foods we cook and crave change accordingly. Life is busy and we can still eat well.

The recipes here are the ones that fill our days. The headnotes and asides include ideas for steps to prep in advance, seasonal swaps, or alternatives for those with dietary restrictions. These are the dishes that I can make ahead for those evenings when we arrive home after soccer practice and everyone is starving, or to give to friends with a new baby. There are meals to pull together on a weeknight after work that can be composed for kids or adults, or to feel proud of when we have an impromptu date with the neighbors. Included are the muffins I hand my kids in the car when we are late getting to school, and the salad dressings that make me happy to be eating a bowl of plants for dinner. Herein lie the cookies I can make from memory for special occasions or just because it's Tuesday, the guacamole Hugh makes every time we buy avocados from Costco and they all turn ripe on the same day, and the Brussels sprouts dish that is requested at every family holiday dinner.

In a time of increasing food intolerances and dietary preferences, "healthy" feels wildly subjective, something only marketing dollars can make us believe is a one-size-fits-all word. These recipes are seasonally minded and invoke feelings of bounty. Some can get you dinner in under thirty minutes, and others require a few hours of simmering on the stove, perfect for a Sunday afternoon, making the house smell dreamy. The breadth we cover in here is reflective of a full life, a meal for all the different kinds of days we have or moods we're in or amount of time we wish to spend in the kitchen.

This is the food that works for us. This is the food that is woven into the course of our crazy, between good intentions and just keeping it together, whether our table is just our family or filled with friends. This is abundance. This is home. This food is my connection to you.

This is the food that brings us around our table.

Equipment

I've kept this list succinct because I find these suggestions from other home cooks can get lengthy and unreasonable. These are my ride-or-die small appliances and tools:

Food Processor: Some will choose a Vitamix to do similar work, but not me. I prefer the round chop to the vortex of a blender, no matter how powerful. Better for sauces, dips, veggie burger dough, things I am making way more often than a smoothie.

Rimmed Baking Sheets, Loaf and Square Baking Pans: I love USA pans. I have phased out my glass dishes because I prefer the straight corners and how they bake. We do our best to not use Teflon materials, so we choose stainless steel, which is a great conductor of heat and easily lined with parchment for baking projects.

Good Knives: A (routinely sharpened!) chef's knife, santoku (another universal cooking knife with a shorter blade than my chef's knife, for more control), paring knife, large and small serrated. All you need!

Kitchen Scissors: Always. I keep one burner pair that my kids inevitably use for crafts and one really nice pair that I treat like a good knife: They never go in the dishwasher and are *not* allowed for crafting.

Dutch Oven: Most used is my 4.5-quart for everyday cooking. I also have a 7-quart and 9-quart for entertaining. Yes, my white ones get dirty, but they look pretty on the stove and clean up easily with a scrub of Bar Keepers Friend. I do not have a slow cooker or Instant Pot because I can do everything those do in my Dutch ovens with more time and less cabinet real estate.

Cookware: I love my All-Clad skillets and pots. I have invested in these over time, and they'll last forever. I use my cast-iron and carbon steel just as often for a great sear on proteins as for a pasta bake or frittata that transfers from stove to oven. They do require slightly more upkeep to not rust. I do keep one ceramic nonstick around for eggs, which gets replaced often because nonstick has a short lifespan, regardless of the brand or how much you spend.

Kitchen-Aid Stand Mixer: Obviously this is another investment piece and not for everyone. I make cookies, cakes, pizza dough, and cinnamon roll dough (I also shred cooked chicken in there with the paddle attachment!), and although those are not daily needs, this piece of equipment is so handy when I do make them.

Rasp Grater / Microplane: I think either lemon zest or grated garlic is called for in 90 percent of the recipes in here. You will definitely need one of these. They don't last forever; you'll want to replace it once the grater gets dull.

Glass Tupperware: Sure, it is heavy, but it washes well and doesn't stain. I keep Weck jars or empty, cleaned jam jars for sauces and large mason jars or similar for gifting granola or soup.

Digital Thermometer: Took me too many years to spend $10 on one of these and stop panicking about undercooked or overcooked chicken.

Oxo Tongs + Earlywood Cooking Sticks: I have a carafe of kitchen tools I try to keep edited, but I could not get by without these two gals. A silicone scraper and large whisk come in a close second.

Mandoline: They make shaved vegetables in salads a uniform thickness, which makes the dish look restaurant quality. I don't use it every day, but when I want paper-thin fennel or onion, there is nothing that does the job better.

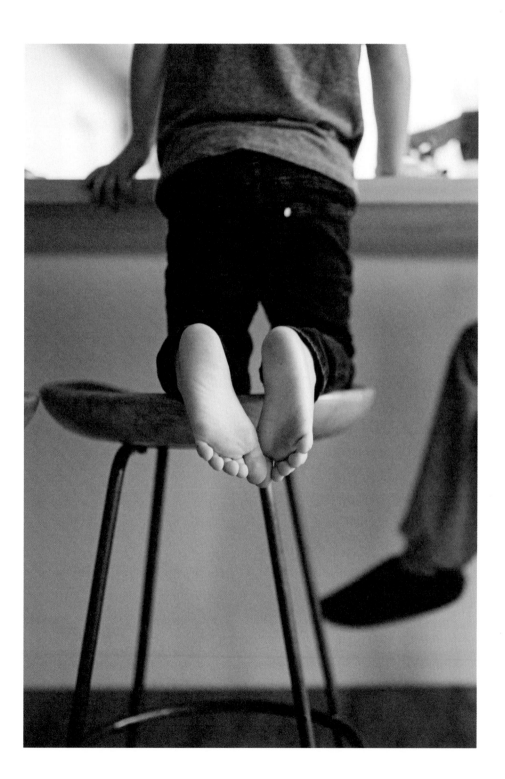

CHAPTER 1

FIRST THING

12   A Crispy Cornmeal Waffle

15   Avocado Toast with Crispy Za'atar Chickpeas

16   Banana Blender Pancakes

20   Breakfast Salad

24   Cinnamon-Apple Baked Oatmeal

27   Broccoli, Caramelized Onion
      + White Cheddar Quiche

31   Granola Number 3

32   Harvest Breakfast Cake

34   Lemon Breakfast Loaf

38   Overnight Oats, Two Ways

43   Pepper + Chorizo Breakfast Bake

44   Pumpkin Muffins with Pepita Crumble

46   A Few Smoothies

48   Sweet Potato Cinnamon Rolls

A Crispy Cornmeal Waffle

If you are looking for quick nutrition and fiber before school, flip ahead to the Overnight Oats (page 38). If you have a little more time and want a weekend brunch hit, this is your waffle!

These waffles get a unique texture from the cornmeal. I knowwwww that whisking up the egg whites is an extra step and dirty dish, but I have found no other way to get the lift and crispness that this step achieves. I have written this recipe with berries, but I've been known to lean savory by adding some shredded cheddar and chives to the batter and topping them with bacon, a fried egg, and hot sauce.

2 large eggs

3 tablespoons / 40 g sugar

Pinch of salt

3 tablespoons / 40 g unsalted butter, warmed

½ teaspoon vanilla extract

1 cup / 240 ml buttermilk

½ cup / 78 g finely ground yellow cornmeal

¾ cup / 90 g cake flour (or all-purpose flour)

1 teaspoon baking powder

½ teaspoon baking soda

12 ounces / 340 g strawberries, trimmed and chopped

Butter and maple syrup

Makes 6–8

Separate the egg yolks from the whites. Whisk the whites into stiff peaks.

In another bowl, whisk together the egg yolks, sugar, salt, butter, and vanilla. Add the buttermilk and whisk to combine. Add the cornmeal, flour, baking powder, and baking soda and fold to combine. Let the batter sit so the cornmeal softens a bit. This would be a good moment to chop up your strawberries. Fold in the egg whites.

Heat your waffle iron. Cook according to instructions. To get crisp edges, avoid overfilling. If you are the short order cook for the morning, sling them onto plates as they're ready, or keep them warm in a low oven.

Serve your warm waffles with butter, maple syrup, and fresh berries (or see the headnote for a savory take!).

CHANGE IT UP
Dairy free: Replace the butter with a plant-based alternative or oil. The buttermilk can be replaced by mixing 1 scant cup / 225 ml of almond or oat milk with a teaspoon of white vinegar.

Avocado Toast with Crispy Za'atar Chickpeas

Most often, my breakfast is an avocado toast, dressed up or dressed down depending on how much time I have. It's nice to have texture and color to make a simple toast more satisfying.

You must start with a good, fresh loaf, so don't undercut this effort with some floppy slice of grocery store bread. Start the chickpeas first, and by the time you whisk up your tahini and pour a coffee, they'll be ready.

I'm able to find these Middle Eastern spices in most well-stocked markets these days, but if you cannot, they are always available online. If you want a shortcut, buy packaged crispy chickpeas, usually near the chips.

1 (15-ounce / 425 g) can of chickpeas, drained

1 tablespoon avocado oil

½ teaspoon sea salt

1 teaspoon za'atar

FOR THE TAHINI DRIZZLE
2 tablespoons tahini

2 tablespoons lemon juice

2 tablespoons water

Pinch of sumac

Big pinch of salt

6 ounces / 170 g cherry tomatoes, chopped

1 clove of garlic, grated

Handful of fresh parsley or cilantro, minced

Extra-virgin olive oil

Zest of 1 lemon

Salt and freshly ground pepper

2 thick slices sourdough or country loaf

1 large avocado

Microgreens

Feta cheese, optional

Makes 2

Preheat the oven to 375 F° / 190°C and line a rimmed baking sheet with parchment paper. Pick through the drained chickpeas and push the beans out of their skins. It doesn't have to be perfect, just get most. Rub them dry on a clean dish cloth.

On the baking sheet, combine the chickpeas, oil, salt, and za'atar and toss to coat. Roast the chickpeas for 35 to 40 minutes, shaking the pan halfway through, until golden and crispy. Let them cool to crisp up.

Mix up your tahini, lemon juice, water, sumac, and salt until smooth. Set aside.

In another bowl, combine the chopped tomatoes with the garlic, herbs, a drizzle of oil, lemon zest, and big pinch of salt and pepper.

Toast your bread. Smash the avocado onto the toast—it's best chunky; don't turn it into a puree. Sprinkle the avocado with salt and pepper. Pile some tomatoes on top, a drizzle of tahini sauce, a handful of crispy chickpeas, some microgreens, and crumbled feta, if using.

Banana Blender Pancakes

My daughter is obsessed with toaster waffles. Every single morning. Unwavering. Too much maple syrup every time. Nothing has the same crunch as a store-bought toaster waffle, but lest I miss them on a grocery run, these pancakes pass her test and are still a good delivery system for all that maple syrup.

You don't have to use a blender, but I find it easier to just whiz it all up in there. I'll even blend the wet ingredients the night before, measure my dry ingredients, and just stir to combine in the morning to make things go quickly.

We want the banana to be extra brown, as it contributes to the sweetness and flavor. If you don't have a dying banana, ⅓ cup / 75 g of pumpkin puree with a little more sugar works well too.

Wheat flour absorbs the extra moisture from the banana. The gluten-free swap below will lead to a slightly gummier texture, but we eat them that way often and no one complains. I add flax for fiber, but they turn out just fine without it if it is not something you keep on hand.

1 small extra-ripe banana
(⅓ cup / 75 g)

1 large egg

2 tablespoons salted butter or oil
+ more for cooking

½ teaspoon vanilla extract

1 cup / 240 ml milk or buttermilk

½ teaspoon cinnamon

1 tablespoon flaxseed meal,
optional

½ cup / 45 g oats

1 tablespoon sugar

Pinch of salt

¾ cup / 85 g white whole-wheat
flour

1½ teaspoons baking powder

Makes 12

Put everything **except** the flour and baking powder into a blender and whiz it up until smooth. Add the flour and baking powder and give it one more whiz, just to combine. If you are using a bowl, mash up the banana really well, whisk in the other wet ingredients, then fold in the dry to combine. Scrape down the sides and let the batter rest a few minutes.

Heat a pan over medium heat and warm a slick of butter or oil to coat the bottom of the pan. Cook small pancakes for about 2 minutes per side, until golden and cooked through. Add more butter or oil to the pan between batches.

Serve them like a line cook to your waiting customers with maple syrup, the mapled berries (opposite), fruit compote, or yogurt. Keep a baking dish of them warm in a 200°F / 100°C oven.

CHANGE IT UP
Gluten free: In place of the wheat flour, use 1 full cup / 90 g oats and ¼ cup / 30 g coconut flour.

Vegan: You can skip the egg and simply expect a denser pancake. For a nondairy buttermilk, use a scant cup / 225 ml of any nondairy milk with a splash of apple cider vinegar.

Waffles: Increase the sugar to 3 tablespoons / 35 g.

Mapled Berries

2 cups / 300 g mixed berries

½ cup / 120 ml maple syrup

1 tablespoon salted butter (or vegan butter)

Dash of vanilla extract

Gently simmer all together over low heat for 10 minutes until the berries are tender and warm. Smash the berries up with a masher or the back of a fork. Start these while you prep and cook the pancakes. It is not jam! It will not thicken.

Breakfast Salad

Let's start with a note of practicality: this recipe has been designed for two servings. That's because there's no chance my kids are eating a salad for breakfast. Nevertheless, there's room for flexibility here. Should your breakfast needs require a more substantial serving, increase the quantity of eggs, or even introduce crispy bacon to the mix.

I double the croutons and keep them for a few meals, so it's worth the step. If you happen to have Mixed Roasted Potatoes (page 131) on hand, those are an excellent sub for the croutons. Though this recipe may involve a few steps, the payoff is considerable. It's versatile enough to be used for a leisurely Sunday-morning breakfast but also possesses the charm to impress an impromptu visitor.

1 pint / 300 g cherry tomatoes

1 tablespoon extra-virgin olive oil

Sea salt and pepper

Aleppo or red pepper flakes

2 cups / 275 g torn bread

Extra-virgin olive oil

2 large eggs

2 cups / 40 g baby kale

1 avocado, sliced

FOR THE VINAIGRETTE

2 tablespoons extra-virgin olive oil

1 teaspoon Dijon mustard

1 tablespoon Green Harissa (page 281) or zhoug sauce

2 tablespoons orange juice

1 teaspoon agave nectar or honey

Salt and pepper

Crumbled goat cheese, optional

Hemp seeds, optional

Serves 2

Preheat the oven to 400°F / 200°C. Line a rimmed baking sheet with parchment paper.

Halve the tomatoes. Toss them in the oil, salt, pepper, and Aleppo pepper. Tip them onto the baking sheet and roast for 20 minutes.

Toss the bread pieces with some olive oil and season with salt and pepper. Spread them on another baking sheet and toast for 12 minutes until dry and crisp on the edges. Remove and set aside.

Bring a pot of water to a gentle boil and prepare a small bowl of ice water. Gently add your two eggs and cook them for exactly 6½ minutes (or 7½ if you like a firm yolk) then drop them in the bowl of ice water. After 5 minutes, peel the eggs and gently split them in half.

While the eggs cook, assemble your salad. Whisk all the dressing ingredients together in a large bowl. Toss the greens with the dressing and divide into two bowls. Top with a handful of croutons, roasted tomatoes, and avocado slices, place an egg on top, and sprinkle with cheese and hemp seeds, if using.

MAKE AHEAD
Roast the tomatoes. You can also bake your croutons a day in advance.

Cinnamon-Apple Baked Oatmeal

My friend and food writer Heidi Swanson turned me on to her baked oatmeal a few years back. Her version is studded with blueberries and a layer of bananas and comes together with pantry staples. I continue to tinker with her base recipe. One of my children won't go for a bowlful of oatmeal, but if it's baked and I rebrand it as warm oatmeal cake, I can sell it!

We don't usually blaze through a full pan of this in one morning, so it's handy that the leftovers warm up beautifully with a touch more milk to rehydrate everything.

3 tablespoons / 40 g unsalted butter

2 apples, cored and finely chopped

Sea salt

1 teaspoon cinnamon, divided

Squeeze of fresh lemon juice

2 cups / 475 ml unsweetened almond milk or alternative

⅓ cup / 80 ml maple syrup

2 tablespoons orange juice

1 teaspoon vanilla extract

1 large egg

2 cups / 178 g old-fashioned oats

¼ cup / 22 g steel cut oats

2 tablespoons flaxseed meal

½ cup / 55 g toasted pecan pieces + more for topping

½ teaspoon baking powder

Sea salt

Serves 6

Warm the butter in a skillet over medium heat. Add the chopped apples and a big pinch of salt and sauté a few minutes. Add ½ teaspoon of the cinnamon, and the lemon juice, and sauté another few minutes until just tender. Set aside to cool.

Preheat the oven to 375°F / 190°C and grease an 8-inch / 20 cm or approximately 2-quart / 1.9-L ovenproof dish.

In a large mixing bowl, whisk together the almond milk, maple syrup, orange juice, vanilla, egg, ½ teaspoon of sea salt, and the remaining ½ teaspoon of cinnamon. Add both oats, flaxseed meal, pecans, and baking powder and stir to combine. Stir in the sautéed apples, including all pan juices. Transfer the mixture to the prepared pan, sprinkle a few extra pecans on top, and bake on the middle rack for 27 to 30 minutes until the center is mostly set. It will continue to set as it rests, so pull it a bit before it's completely firm.

Remove to cool slightly. Serve warm, with a little extra milk on top.

CHANGE IT UP
Vegan: You can use coconut oil to sauté the apples. The egg here helps it all hold shape, but it can be replaced with one small mashed overripe banana to achieve the same effect.

If you want to elevate this lovely bowl of oats, drizzle some of the Vegan Coconut Caramel on page 247 over the top!

MAKE AHEAD
Sauté the apples up to a day in advance.

Broccoli, Caramelized Onion + White Cheddar Quiche

I have found that a quiche is a great item to deliver to friends with a new baby because you can enjoy it at all times of the day, and with one hand if you're cradling a baby in the other. It's also a go-to for a brunch or holiday as it can be made completely in advance.

I often use a premade pie crust, and there are great gluten-free ones available, but when I have the time, this hash-brown option is my favorite.

FOR THE CRUST

2 large russet potatoes, peeled

1 tablespoon avocado or olive oil

2 tablespoons all-purpose flour or cornstarch

½ teaspoon sea salt

FOR THE ONIONS

1 tablespoon avocado oil

1 small yellow onion, diced

½ teaspoon sea salt

¼ teaspoon freshly ground pepper

2 teaspoons white wine vinegar

10 ounces / 300 g broccoli florets, steamed and well chopped

Preheat the oven to 350°F / 180°C. Grease a 10-inch / 25 cm ovenproof skillet or cast-iron pan.

Grate the potatoes on the large holes of a box grater. Collect them in a dish towel and wring out all the excess moisture. You should have about 3 to 4 cups of grated potatoes. In a large mixing bowl, combine the potatoes, oil, flour, and salt and stir until the flour is evenly distributed. Press the grated potatoes into the prepared skillet to make your own crust, down the bottom and up the sides, pressing into the elbows of the pan. It will shrink as it bakes. Bake for 35 minutes until golden on the edges. Remove to cool. Leave the oven on.

While the crust cooks, start the onions. Heat the oil in a medium skillet over medium heat. Add the onions, salt, and pepper and sauté until softened, about 5 minutes. Stir in the vinegar. Turn the heat to medium-low and cook, stirring occasionally, until golden, about 20 minutes. When the pan starts to dry up and the onions are getting too dark, add a splash of water. Once the onions are caramelized, set them aside to cool.

Chop the cooled broccoli florets into tiny pieces.

CONTINUED

FOR THE FILLING

5 large eggs

1 cup / 240 ml whole milk

2 teaspoons hot sauce

½ teaspoon sea salt

½ teaspoon freshly ground pepper

Tiny pinch of turmeric (for color)

1½ cups / 170 g grated white cheddar

Mixed greens

Double Mustard Maple Dressing (page 289)

Serves 6

Whisk the eggs. Add the milk, hot sauce, salt, pepper, turmeric, and half the cheese and whisk again.

Sprinkle a layer of cheese on the bottom of the crust. Distribute the chopped broccoli and caramelized onions and pour the egg mixture over the top. Sprinkle the remaining cheese over the top. Bake on the middle rack for 35 minutes or until the center is mostly set (it will be tender and will continue to set as it cools!). Let sit for at least 30 minutes before slicing.

Serve with greens dressed with Double Mustard Maple Dressing.

CHANGE IT UP

You can add ½ pound / 225 g cooked and crumbled bacon, change the cheese, make two and freeze or gift one, but always serve it with some dressed greens on the side for freshness and crunch.

MAKE AHEAD

This can be made up to 2 days in advance and covered and reheated in a 300°F / 150°C oven. To freeze, wrap tightly in plastic wrap after it is cooked and cooled, and store in the freezer for up to 3 months.

Granola Number 3

This is my third cookbook and therefore, third granola recipe in print. This one has just the right amount of sweetness, is flexible while still being specific, and has no dried fruit, as I'll always prefer a load of fresh berries in my bowl instead. Add dried cherries or chopped dates after baking if you disagree.

This makes a sizable amount of granola. It stores well for about a month; gifts perfectly in a glass jar for teachers, coaches, new neighbors, et cetera; and is easily halved if those things are not part of your reality at the moment. However, we always manage to finish a batch within a month even without sharing. Coconut oil is listed here, but olive oil or avocado oil work just as well.

½ cup / 120 ml maple syrup

2 tablespoons sugar

½ cup / 120 ml coconut oil, warmed to liquid

1 teaspoon vanilla extract

1 teaspoon cinnamon

1 teaspoon sea salt

3½ cups / 283 g old-fashioned rolled oats

2 cups / 120 g unsweetened coconut chips (not the thin shreds!)

2 cups / 250 g raw nuts and seeds of your choice (usually almonds and pumpkin seeds for us)

Makes about 6 cups / 675 g

Preheat the oven to 325°F / 165°C. Line two rimmed baking sheets with parchment paper.

In a large mixing bowl, stir together the maple syrup, sugar, coconut oil, vanilla, cinnamon, and salt. Add the oats, coconut chips, and nuts and stir well until everything is coated.

Divide the mixture between the baking sheets, spreading it into the corners in as even a layer as possible.

Bake the granola, stirring every 15 minutes and rotating the pans once halfway through baking, for 35 to 40 minutes. It should look golden brown and toasty. Remove to cool; it will dry to a crisp as it cools.

Allow it to cool completely before transferring it to airtight containers. The granola will last for a few weeks.

Harvest Breakfast Cake

I don't want to send you out for another flour, but cake flour lends a more delicate crumb to baked goods. If you're making a grocery list, add it, but this was also tested with all-purpose flour and works beautifully with that too.

You want two heaping cups of shredded produce total. You can replace whatever you don't have or like with an equal volume of another from the list.

When I say "well-chopped walnuts," I don't mean the texture of almond meal but closer to the small, crunchy bits you'd put on a salad. I just use a knife, but if you prefer a food processor, pulse pieces about 3–4 times until it looks like small pebbles. We want some tooth to it.

I hesitate to put a frosting on a breakfast cake, but a dollop of vanilla Greek yogurt hits the spot.

⅔ cup / 133 g sugar

2 large eggs

½ cup / 112 g plain yogurt

1 teaspoon vanilla extract

Zest of 1 small orange

⅔ cup / 160 ml extra-virgin olive, avocado, or coconut oil

1½ cups / 180 g cake flour

1½ teaspoons baking powder

½ teaspoon baking soda

Sea salt

¾ teaspoon pumpkin pie spice or cinnamon

½ cup / 55 g well-chopped walnuts (see headnote) + more to top

½ cup / 50 g shredded unsweetened coconut

1 cup / 130 g grated zucchini (1 medium)

1 cup / 100 g grated carrot (1 medium)

½ cup / 65 g grated apple (1 small cored apple)

Coarse sugar, to top

Makes 1 (8-inch) cake

Preheat the oven to 350°F / 180°C and line an 8-inch / 20 cm square pan with a parchment paper sling and spray or rub with oil.

In a large bowl or stand mixer with the paddle attachment, combine the sugar, eggs, and yogurt and beat until pale and fluffy. Add the vanilla, orange zest, and oil and mix again. Add the flour, baking powder, baking soda, salt, pie spice or cinnamon, walnuts, and coconut and give it all a few folds. Add the zucchini, carrot, and apple and fold again.

Tip the batter into your prepared pan, sprinkle some walnuts and coarse sugar on top, and bake on the middle rack for 40 to 45 minutes, until a toothpick inserted in the center comes out clean.

Let the cake rest for 10 minutes, then pull the sling out and let the cake cool on a wire rack. Do not slice until completely cool!

The cake will keep at room temperature for a day or two, or covered in the fridge for up to a week.

Lemon Breakfast Loaf

Our house loves a loaf cake, the perfect sweet with coffee or as part of a breakfast spread. Rubbing the lemon zest into the sugar releases the natural oils for a lemonier flavor. You can also do this whole recipe in a stand mixer and just run the sugar and lemon zest for a few minutes before adding everything else. The poppy seeds, should you choose to go for them, add a classic speckle to the loaf while also contributing the slightest crunch in each bite.

Since this is a gluten-free loaf, it's important to get lots of air in the eggs for a fluffy texture. Don't skip on whisking the eggs and sugar for the full two minutes as instructed.

FOR THE LOAF
¾ cup / 150 g sugar

½ teaspoon sea salt

Zest from 2 lemons

3 large eggs

1 tablespoon fresh lemon juice

1 teaspoon lemon extract

½ cup / 120 ml extra-virgin olive oil

½ cup / 112 g plain yogurt, or coconut yogurt

1 cup / 96 g almond flour

½ cup / 70 g superfine brown rice flour

½ cup / 60 g oat flour

2 tablespoons poppy seeds, optional

¼ teaspoon baking soda

2¼ teaspoons baking powder

FOR THE GLAZE
1½ cups / 220 g powdered sugar

2 tablespoons fresh lemon juice

Makes 1 (9-by-5-inch / 23-by-12 cm) loaf

Preheat the oven to 350°F / 180°C and line a loaf pan with a parchment paper sling, leaving a bit of extra paper on two sides for easy removal. Grease the parchment and set aside.

In a large mixing bowl (or stand mixer with paddle attachment), combine the sugar, salt, and lemon zest. Rub the zest into the sugar with your fingertips for about a minute. That smell, so dreamy! Add the lemon juice, extract, and eggs and whisk very well to get some lift, about two minutes. Add the oil and yogurt and whisk everything together to mix.

Add the almond flour, rice flour, oat flour, poppy seeds (if using), baking soda, and baking powder. Stir everything until just combined. Transfer to your prepared pan and bake on the middle rack for 45 to 50 minutes until a toothpick inserted in the center comes out clean.

While the loaf bakes, stir together the powdered sugar and lemon juice until smooth. Once the cake has cooled, drizzle the glaze over the top.

Slice it into thick slices—she's too delicate for thin, whimsy slices—and serve with plain yogurt and berries. Or toast the slices for more texture!

CHANGE IT UP
I buy superfine brown rice flour online or at Whole Foods. I like the texture of these flours for a gluten-free loaf, but you can swap one or all of them with a gluten-free 1:1 flour (e.g., Bob's Red Mill, King Arthur, or Cup4Cup). If gluten is not an issue, use 1¾ cups / 210 g all-purpose flour.

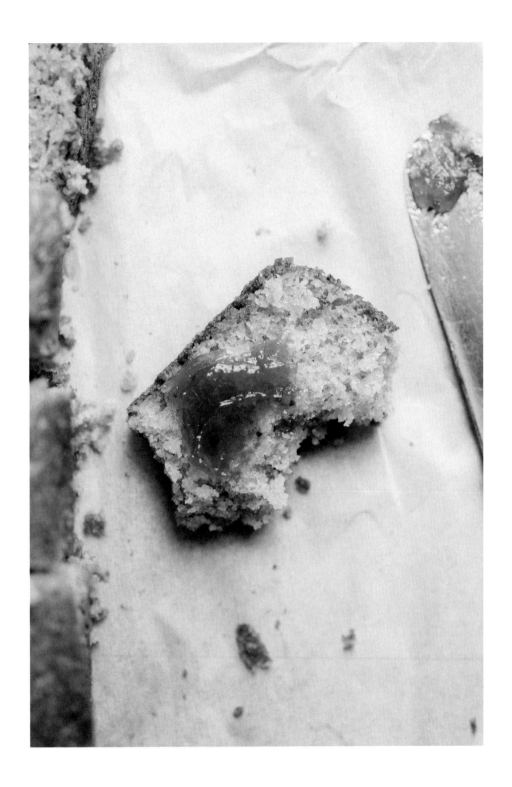

Overnight Oats, Two Ways

My early bird likes to eat breakfast immediately upon waking. There is no waiting around for eggs or breakfast sausage—those can be second breakfast. He will patter down to the kitchen and go straight for cereal. I can intercept his routine with a note that these oats are waiting in the fridge.

My late bird, who often needs to eat on the car ride to school, also likes overnight oats, but of a different variety. So, here are two versions. It just wouldn't be right if they both liked the same flavor of overnight oats. These are best the next day but can be enjoyed for up to three days if kept in the fridge. These are an easy, entry-level recipe to get kids in the kitchen if you're looking to get them involved.

1 cup / 224 g plain yogurt

1½ cups / 360 ml milk or alternative

½ cup / 120 ml orange juice

¼ cup / 60 ml maple syrup

½ teaspoon vanilla extract

2 tablespoons cocoa powder

2 cups / 180 g old-fashioned oats

1 tablespoon flaxseed meal

1 tablespoon chia seeds

1 pint / 300 g of mixed berries, chopped small, divided

Makes 4–6 small jars

Curran's Cocoa Berry Oats

In a large mixing bowl, combine the yogurt, milk, orange juice, maple syrup, vanilla, and cocoa powder and whisk to combine.

Add the oats, flaxseed meal, chia, and half the berries and stir to combine. Transfer the mixture to individual containers or jars (it will look loose, but the chia absorbs moisture overnight). Top with the remaining berries and store in the fridge overnight.

1 cup / 224 g plain yogurt

1½ cups / 360 ml milk or alternative

½ cup / 120 ml orange juice

¼ cup / 60 ml maple syrup

½ teaspoon vanilla extract

½ teaspoon ground cinnamon

1 apple, grated (1 cup / 130 g)

1 medium carrot, finely grated (½ cup / 55 g)

½ cup / 75 g golden raisins

⅓ cup / 30 g finely shredded coconut

1 tablespoon flaxseed meal

2 cups / 180 g old-fashioned oats

½ cup / 65 g chopped mixed nuts and seeds, divided (sunflower, almonds, pecans, etc.)

Makes 4–6 small jars

Cleo's Morning Glory Oats

In a large mixing bowl, combine the yogurt, milk, orange juice, maple syrup, vanilla, and cinnamon and whisk to combine.

Add the apple, carrot, raisins, coconut, flaxseed meal, oats, and half of the nuts and seeds. Stir again to mix. Transfer the porridge into individual containers, sprinkle the remaining nuts and seeds over the top, and store in the fridge for at least an hour, ideally overnight.

CHANGE IT UP

Dairy free: A coconut or almond-based yogurt and milk will keep these dairy free!

Pepper + Chorizo Breakfast Bake

Quite often in my adult life, I have found the need for an egg-dish recipe large enough for a group: Christmas morning, a bridal shower, moms' group, office breakfast, and Father's Day brunch to name a few. Not to mention for those mornings when you need something handheld to take with you to work or school—slabs of the frittata are perfect between a toasted English muffin.

Chorizo can be pretty spicy, so to keep it kid friendly, we're not using a ton here. You could use some cooked and crumbled bacon or breakfast sausage in its place for something more mild.

10 large eggs, room temperature

2 tablespoons sour cream

½ cup / 120 ml whole milk

Dash of hot sauce + more for serving

Salt and pepper

1 tablespoon olive oil

2 cups / 260 g peeled, chopped sweet potato (1 medium)

½ an onion, chopped

Salt and pepper

6 ounces / 170 g chorizo

1 bell pepper, chopped small

4 ounces / 113 g baby kale or spinach, chopped

Handful of cherry tomatoes, chopped

2 cups / 227 g shredded pepper jack cheese, optional

Cilantro

Avocado

Serves 6

In a large mixing bowl, whisk up the eggs, sour cream, milk, hot sauce, and a few big pinches of salt and pepper. Set aside.

Preheat the oven to 350°F / 180°C and grease a 12-inch / 30 cm ovenproof skillet or an 8-by-11-inch (roughly 2-quart / 20-by-28 cm) baking dish.

In your skillet, heat the oil over medium heat. Add the sweet potatoes, onions, and a pinch of salt and pepper and sauté. Cover and cook about 10 minutes until just tender. Add the chorizo, breaking it up with your cooking utensil, and bell pepper and sauté again until tender. Add a bit more oil if the pan looks dry. Add the greens and tomatoes and stir a few times to wilt. If you are baking it in this same skillet, sprinkle half of the cheese on top of the vegetables, pour the egg mixture on top, then finish with the remaining cheese. Alternatively, transfer it all to your prepared baking dish.

Cover the pan and bake for 20 minutes. Turn the heat up to 375°F / 190°C, uncover, and bake for another 15 to 20 minutes until just set and the top is golden. Let it rest for 10 minutes before cutting. Serve slices with fresh herbs and avocado.

CHANGE IT UP
Dairy free: Use a plain, nondairy creamer in place of the milk, and skip the sour cream and cheese. Serve it with some chunky guacamole.

Vegetarian: I can find the vegan alternative of chorizo in most markets, so this is easy to keep vegetarian.

MAKE AHEAD
Sauté your veggies and whisk up your egg-and-milk/cream mixture up to a day in advance. Wait to combine until you are ready to bake.

Pumpkin Muffins with Pepita Crumble

Some version of this recipe has lived on the Sprouted Kitchen blog for years as I have tinkered with it to finally arrive on this delicate but comforting final result. These are muffins that taste more like breakfast than a dessert, but that said, we often add mini chocolate chips. The crumble dresses them up a bit, or sometimes my daughter will forgo an extra dirty bowl and just top with rainbow sprinkles for flair.

FOR THE CRUMBLE

⅓ cup (56 g) pepitas, roughly chopped

½ cup (50 g) almond flour

⅓ cup (30 g) rolled oats

¼ teaspoon cinnamon

¼ cup (55 g) light brown sugar

¼ cup (½ stick) / 56 g cold unsalted butter (or vegan butter), cut into pieces

FOR THE MUFFINS

2 large eggs, room temperature

1 cup (255 g) pumpkin puree

1 teaspoon pure vanilla extract

½ cup (108 g) melted coconut oil (or avocado oil or melted butter)

⅔ cup (145 g) light brown sugar

1¼ teaspoons pumpkin pie spice

½ teaspoons sea salt

1½ cups (150 g) almond flour

½ cup (75 g) superfine brown rice or oat flour

¼ cup (30 g) tapioca starch

1½ teaspoons baking powder

½ teaspoon baking soda

Makes 12

Preheat the oven to 375°F / 190°C and line or grease a muffin tin. Set aside.

In a medium bowl, combine the pepitas, almond flour, oats, cinnamon, brown sugar, and butter and smoosh everything together with your hands to make a crumbly mixture. Since the butter is cold, you should have pea-size pieces. Set aside in the fridge until you're ready to assemble.

In a medium mixing bowl with a hand mixer, or in the bowl of an electric mixer, beat the eggs on medium speed for 3 minutes until pale yellow and very frothy. Add the pumpkin puree and mix well to combine. Add the vanilla, coconut oil, light brown sugar, pumpkin pie spice, and salt and mix again. Slowly add the almond flour, brown rice flour, tapioca starch, baking powder, and baking soda and, using a silicone spatula, fold the dry ingredients in to combine. The batter will be quite thick. Let it rest for 20 minutes.

Fill the muffin tins three-quarters of the way full and top with the crumble mixture, pressing it lightly into the top. Pop in the muffins and then turn the heat down to 350°F / 180°C. Bake on the middle rack of the oven for 35 minutes, rotating the pan halfway through. Remove and cool completely.

The muffins will last at room temperature for 2 days and kept in the fridge for up to a week. They also freeze well!

CHANGE IT UP

As written, the muffins are gluten free and only lightly sweetened. If you do not need or want the muffins to be gluten free, replace the almond, rice, and tapioca flours with 2 cups / 272 g all-purpose flour.

A Few Smoothies

Smoothies have become a go-to after-school snack for the kids and their friends, or a "bridge snack" as they call it. This is a hit list of our favorites. I try to bulk up ours with greens, frozen cauliflower, or berries, which are naturally low in sugar. I adjust here to taste; I am happy with half a frozen banana and double the greens, whereas my kids prefer the opposite ratio. If the kids' friends are over, I'll add a big squeeze of honey too, since I'm in the business of making sure they like eating here. In a decent blender, the greens will pulverize well and really only compromise the color, not the flavor, making it a great way to sneak more nutrition into pickier kids.

As I am always overbuying bananas, I peel and freeze ones that are getting speckled, so I have them on hand. Frozen over fresh helps thicken the smoothie.

Each smoothie makes one large or two small smoothies. Just toss everything into the blender until smooth.

Each serves 1–2

Aloha Greens

1 cup / 170 g pineapple pieces

1 cup / 210 g frozen mango

1 frozen banana

2 handfuls of baby spinach

1 scoop vanilla protein powder

1 cup / 240 ml coconut water

1 cup / 240 ml coconut milk

Chocolate Dreams

1 frozen banana

1¼ cups / 360 ml oat or nut milk

2 tablespoons cocoa powder

2 dates, pitted

2 tablespoons natural nut butter

Handful of spinach

Pep-Start Shake

1 frozen banana

Squeeze of honey

2 tablespoons almond butter

1 scoop of protein or collagen powder

½ cup / 120 ml leftover coffee

½ cup / 120 ml coconut milk

2 tablespoons hemp seeds

Berry Breakfast Smoothie

1 frozen banana

1 cup / 160 g frozen berries

2 tablespoons almond butter

¼ cup / 23 g oats

2 tablespoons flaxseed meal, hemp, or chia seeds

2 dates, pitted

2 cups / 475 ml unsweetened nut milk

Feel-Good Green Smoothie

1 cup / 110 g frozen riced cauliflower

2 dates, pitted

1 stalk of celery

2 pears or apples, cored and chopped

1 handful of baby kale

3 tablespoons / 30 g hemp seeds

3 tablespoons / 16 g pumpkin seeds

1-inch / 2.5 cm knob of fresh ginger, peeled and chopped

Squeeze of fresh lemon

A couple of mint leaves

2 cups / 475 ml coconut water

Sweet Potato Cinnamon Rolls

In case you read nothing else, these need to be started the day before you want to eat them! With proofing in the fridge, you could even start them two days in advance.

We eat pretty healthily in our house, whatever that means these days, but there is only so much I can do to lighten up a cinnamon roll before it's just not worth making. This recipe makes just a few alterations to a classic recipe, replacing some of the butter with sweet potato puree and adding some spelt to the all-purpose flour for fiber and whole grain flavor, but otherwise, they are the real deal. That said, using all-purpose flour entirely is absolutely fine.

I love it when my kids request a special dish that we "always have" on a holiday—and this is it for Christmas morning. These are rich and delicious and perfect for a special occasion. The rolls have a couple of windows of rest and rise time. Start the dough at least the afternoon before you are planning to enjoy them. I bake them in a 12-inch / 30 cm cast-iron pan, but you could also get twelve slightly thinner rolls in a 9-by-13-inch / 23-by-33 cm baking dish.

½ cup / 120 ml whole milk, barely warmed, not hot

1¼ teaspoons active dry yeast

¼ cup / 85 g honey

½ cup / 60 g spelt flour (or whole-wheat pastry flour)

2 large eggs, room temperature

2¼ cups / 361 g unbleached all-purpose flour + more as needed

½ teaspoon fine sea salt

6 tablespoons / 84 g unsalted butter, cubed, room temperature

½ cup / 164 g sweet potato puree (from 1 medium baked potato)

FOR THE FILLING

3 tablespoons / 42 g unsalted butter, room temperature

½ teaspoon sea salt

½ cup / 110 g light brown sugar

2 teaspoons cinnamon

Day before baking

In a stand mixer with the paddle attachment, combine the milk, yeast, honey, and spelt flour. Mix on low until well combined and resembling a loose pancake batter. Cover with a dish towel and let it sit for an hour.

Once the dough has rested, using the dough hook, add the eggs, then the all-purpose flour and salt and mix for 5 to 6 minutes. The dough should start to pull away from the sides at this point, but it will be sticky. While the mixer is still going, drop in the butter and potato puree, and mix until well incorporated. Mix for another minute. The dough should hold together like a loose ball. If the dough looks a little wet, add flour, 1 tablespoon at a time, until it holds together. It should still be pretty sticky and will be easier to work with after it chills.

Scrape the dough into a large, greased bowl, rolling it around a few times to grease the outside. Cover and let it rest in the fridge for 12 to 24 hours.

While it rests, make your filling. Combine the butter, salt, brown sugar, and cinnamon, and mix. Set aside.

FOR THE GLAZE

4 tablespoons / 56 g unsalted butter

4 ounces / 113 g cream cheese, room temperature

⅔ cup / 75 g powdered sugar

¼ cup / 80 ml maple syrup

1 teaspoon vanilla extract

1 teaspoon orange zest

Pinch of salt

½ cup / 60 g toasted pecan pieces, coarsely chopped + more for garnish

Makes 10 rolls

Make your glaze (this may also be done days in advance and kept in the fridge). Brown the butter in a small pan by warming it over medium heat, stirring frequently, until it smells nutty and the color begins to turn amber, about 5 minutes. If your pan is dark, use a spoon to check the color. We're looking for a light amber. Pull from the heat to cool completely.

Get the mixer going with the paddle attachment. Add the cream cheese and whip that for a minute. Add the cooled butter and mix again, scraping down the sides. Slowly add the powdered sugar, maple syrup, vanilla, orange zest, and salt and mix well until smooth, scraping down the sides as needed. Set aside.

Day of baking

Turn out the cold dough onto a clean, lightly floured surface and knead it a few times. Let it sit for 15 minutes. Roll it into a 20-by-12-inch / 50-by-30 cm rectangle. Spread the filling over the dough, leaving a ½-inch / 1.25 cm border around all sides. Sprinkle the pecans over the filling. Roll the dough into a long tube and slice the roll into 10 rolls. Generously grease a 12-inch / 30 cm round ovenproof dish (cast iron works great) and arrange the rolls. They'll look small in the pan, but don't worry, they'll grow. Let them rest for 1 to 2 hours, covered with a dish cloth, to rise again. We want them to double in size. You can also leave them assembled in the fridge overnight and bring them to room temperature before baking.

Preheat the oven to 350°F / 180°C. Bake the rolls for 20 to 22 minutes until fluffy and browned on top. (If you're precise, about 190°F / 88°C in the center of the roll.) Remove to cool.

When they are no longer piping hot, spread the glaze over the top and sprinkle with more pecans. Enjoy warm.

CHAPTER 2

SNACKS + STARTERS

54	Beet Dip
57	Hugh's Guacamole
58	Smoky Eggplant Dip
61	Whipped Feta with Crushed Olives
62	Tropical Pico
64	Rosemary Nut + Pretzel Mix
69	Mushroom Quesadillas with Sunflower Seed Crema
70	White Bean Bruschetta
73	Butternut + Chorizo Flatbread with Pepita Pesto
74	Pizza Knots
77	Halloumi Skewers with Nectarines + Mint Chimichurri
78	Grilled Peach + Burrata Salad with Breadcrumb Crispies
81	After-School Banana Chocolate Chip Chunkers
82	Blackberry Gin Spritz
85	Watermelon Margaritas
87	Beachside Mai Tais

Beet Dip

I am always looking for things to dip fresh, toasty bread into. If you are not a beet person, flip to the next recipe because this dip makes no effort to hide beets' "beet-iness."

To streamline the cooking time, it is best to use beets similar in size. If you have a big variance, pull the smaller ones sooner than the instructed time, and leave larger ones in a little longer. You want to test them with a knife and be able to pierce through to the center with ease. Your shortcut here is to use those pre-steamed packs you can get in most produce sections. Since the prepackaged beets tend to be smaller, I suggest four instead of the two this recipe calls for. Pomegranate molasses is a bit tricky to find, but if you don't stock that, use honey as a sweetener here.

2 medium beets
(about ½ pound / 225 g,
or 6 ounces / 170 g
pre-cooked)

2 tablespoons minced shallot
(half of a small)

1 teaspoon white miso paste

1 tablespoon pomegranate
molasses or honey

½ cup / 60 g lightly toasted
walnuts + more for garnish

1 tablespoon extra-virgin
olive oil

1 teaspoon Dijon mustard

½ teaspoon dried oregano

¼ cup / 15 g fresh chopped chives
+ more for garnish

1 teaspoon sea salt

2 tablespoons lemon juice

3 ounces / 85 g goat cheese,
room temperature

Flaky salt

Za'atar

Crackers or naan

Serves 4–6

Preheat the oven to 400°F / 200°C.

Scrub and trim the beets, composting the greens or saving them for another use. Give the beets a prick all over with a fork, then put them in a small baking dish and fill the dish with an inch of water. Cover tightly with foil and bake for 45 to 55 minutes, or until the beets can be pierced easily with a knife. Remove and let cool.

Peel the skins off the beets, and quarter them. In a food processor, combine the beets, shallot, miso, pomegranate molasses, and walnuts and pulse a few times until the mixture is pebbly. Add the oil, Dijon, dried oregano, chives, salt, lemon juice, and goat cheese and run again until mostly smooth. Transfer to a bowl and cover. Chill in the fridge for an hour for the flavors to blend.

Garnish with another handful of walnuts, fresh chives, flaky salt, and a sprinkle of za'atar and serve with crackers or naan.

CHANGE IT UP
Have leftovers? It's a great spread for a veggie sandwich.

Dairy free: Skip the goat cheese and add ¼ cup / 30 g more walnuts.

Hugh's Guacamole

I do a majority of the cooking in our house, but Hugh excels at three family staples because his attention to detail is exponentially better than mine: coffee, eggs, and guacamole. I will never measure my coffee beans or moderate the temperature of the water I pour over the grounds. My scrambled eggs never look as pillowy as his, and he is extremely selective about the ripeness of avocados he'll use for guacamole. This is nothing you haven't heard before, but his guac is always the most popular appetizer or snack.

The heat of the guacamole will depend on your jalapeño. We include some seeds, as jalapeños are pretty mild, but you can remove all of them if you prefer your guac on the mild side. This amount is a perfect snack for our family, but double it if you have guests or a taco party planned.

1 large clove garlic

2 tablespoons finely minced red onion

1 small jalapeño, finely minced

3 tablespoons / 45 ml lime juice

1 teaspoon sea salt, to taste

Freshly ground pepper

3 medium or 2 large avocados

¼ cup / 5 g chopped cilantro

Serves 4

Into a mixing bowl, grate the garlic on a rasp grater. Add the onion, jalapeño, lime juice, salt, and pepper. Pit and cube the avocados, then add them and the cilantro to the bowl. Smash the mixture with the back of a fork until chunky but well mixed. We don't want smooth and even; we're going for rustic. Taste for salt. Serve immediately.

ON AVOCADO RIPENESS
The perfect avocado for guacamole feels like an old softball. Firm, but a little bit of give when you grip it in your hands. Avocados may be available year-round, but they are without question best in spring and summer.

Smoky Eggplant Dip

This is essentially the Middle Eastern dip baba ghanoush, with a few additions. We love this as a dip with pita chips, or as part of a Mediterranean-themed bowl bar. It could even tick toward an eggplant hummus with a can of drained chickpeas and more tahini whizzed in.

Aleppo pepper has a bit more depth than cayenne, but it is trickier to find. We just need a touch of heat, so use either.

If you have a smoker, smoke the eggplants for extra flavor! If you have neither the appliance nor the time, char the eggplants over a gas stove top (messy but effective), or char them in a hot oven for the same effect.

2 large eggplants

2 cloves garlic

3 tablespoons / 45 ml extra-virgin olive oil + more as needed

3 tablespoons / 45 ml lemon juice

Dash of red wine vinegar

¼ cup / 5 g finely chopped parsley + more for garnish

¼ cup / 5 g finely chopped cilantro

¼ cup / 64 g tahini

1–2 tablespoons pomegranate molasses or honey

1 teaspoon cumin

¼ teaspoon smoked paprika + more for garnish

Pinch of Aleppo pepper or cayenne

1 teaspoon sea salt, to taste

Freshly ground pepper

Sesame seeds, for garnish

Serves 4-6

Preheat the oven to 475°F / 245°C. Lightly oil the eggplants and pop them on a rimmed baking sheet and bake for 20 minutes until totally charred and collapsed onto themselves. Add the garlic cloves in the last 5 minutes, just to take the raw edge off them.

Let the eggplant cool enough to handle. Pull it in half and scoop out the flesh, leaving the burnt skin behind, and transfer it to a mixing bowl or food processor. If yours looks watery, leave it in a fine-mesh strainer for a bit, to drain off the extra water.

Finely grate or mince the garlic. Into the mixing bowl, add the mashed eggplant, garlic, oil, lemon juice, vinegar, parsley, cilantro, tahini, pomegranate molasses to taste, cumin, smoked paprika, Aleppo pepper, salt, and lots of pepper. Mash everything around to incorporate until mostly smooth. Alternatively, give it a few pulses in a food processor.

Serve with a sprinkle of parsley and sesame seeds on top.

Whipped Feta with Crushed Olives

I used to whip feta with milk, but the site Serious Eats taught me about using Greek yogurt, which yields a super creamy, pillowy dip. Serve it with warm pita or grilled sourdough and some cucumbers sliced on an extreme bias. I'm not usually one to suggest more prep time, but homemade pita is immeasurably better and there are plenty of great recipes online.

I like the presentation of the salty bits on top, but you can pulse all the ingredients together for a more homogeneous texture.

8 ounces / 225 g sheep's milk feta cheese

½ cup / 114 g plain Greek yogurt

1 clove garlic, chopped

Freshly ground pepper

4 ounces / 113 g mixed pitted olives

3 ounces / 85 g sundried tomatoes

1 clove garlic, minced

1 tablespoon lemon zest

Squeeze of fresh lemon juice

Pinch of red pepper flakes

½ cup / 10 g chopped flat-leaf parsley

Few sprigs of mint leaves, chopped

Extra-virgin olive oil

Toasted pine nuts

Warm, torn pita or grilled bread

Persian cucumbers, sliced on a diagonal

Serves 6

In a food processor, combine the feta, yogurt, garlic, and a few grinds of pepper. Pulse until smooth and fluffy, about a minute. If it's dry and too thick to move, add a drizzle of olive oil and whip again.

Plate the dip in a shallow bowl with some swoops of a spoon for the topping to fall into.

Smash the olives with the side of your knife, give them a rough chop, and collect them in a mixing bowl. Mince the sundried tomatoes, then add those, the garlic, lemon zest, lemon juice, pepper flakes, a few grinds of freshly ground pepper, parsley, mint, and a drizzle of olive oil. Toss it all together to combine. Spoon it over your whipped feta, along with all the juicy bits.

Top with toasted pine nuts and serve with bread and cucumber slices.

MAKE AHEAD
Both the feta and olive components can be made a day in advance, but for better presentation, assemble just before serving.

Tropical Pico

We love this salsa in fish tacos, on top of Blackened Salmon (page 138), or with the Mushroom "Carnitas" (page 187). If you want to serve it on its own, adding two cubed avocados helps make it a more substantial appetizer with chips. Not to put pressure on your knife skills, but the smaller you can get the produce, the better.

The acidity in the pineapple breaks down the other ingredients, so this is best eaten within a day or two.

2 cups / 330 g chopped
fresh pineapple

1 ripe mango, diced small

1 Roma tomato, seeded and
chopped

1 bundle cilantro, chopped

¼ of a red onion, minced

1 serrano, seeded to taste
and minced

1 lime, zest and juice

½ teaspoon sea salt

A few grinds of freshly
ground pepper

Pinch of sugar

Makes 3 cups / 475 ml

Put all the ingredients in a bowl and mix to combine. Keep covered in the fridge until ready to use.

Rosemary Nut + Pretzel Mix

A perfect bar snack: sweet and salty and crunchy and easy to make in advance. This is a great mix for an after-school snack or something to leave on the counter for friends while you're pulling dinner together.

Feel free to swap your nuts; just keep the same quantity overall. If your oven does not go down to 200°F / 100°C for that second bake time, crack the door open a small bit to cool it down yourself.

1 egg white

2 teaspoons water

¾ teaspoon sea salt

Freshly ground pepper

1 teaspoon garlic powder

½ teaspoon paprika

Pinch of cayenne

2 teaspoons fennel seeds, slightly crushed

2 teaspoons fresh orange zest

2 tablespoons fresh rosemary, roughly chopped

⅓ cup / 37 g powdered sugar

2 cups / 198 g raw pecan halves

½ cup / 50 g raw walnut halves

1 cup / 120 g raw cashews

Big handful of salted pretzel sticks

Makes 4 cups / 1 L

Preheat the oven to 250°F / 120°C and line a rimmed baking sheet with parchment paper.

With a stand or electric mixer, whisk the egg white and water until just fluffy. Add the salt, pepper, garlic powder, paprika, cayenne, fennel, orange zest, and fresh rosemary and give it one more whip. Add the sugar and whisk once more to incorporate.

Add the pecans, walnuts, and cashews and give them a few stirs to coat. Spread them out on the prepared baking sheet and bake for 30 minutes. Turn the heat down to 200°F / 100°C, give everything a stir, and cook another 20 minutes. The nuts will come out a bit tacky but will crisp up as they cool. Set aside to cool completely. Toss in the pretzel sticks.

The mix can be stored in an airtight container or bag for a week, or frozen for a few months.

Mushroom Quesadillas with Sunflower Seed Crema

For these delicious quesadillas, you'll need a batch of the Mushroom "Carnitas" on page 187. Start soaking your sunflower seeds, make the mushrooms, prep your other ingredients, and finish with the crema. It sounds complicated, but work smart and you can still make these quickly.

Between the smashed potato, those savory mushrooms, and this delicious crema, we are not talking about scraping together kids' cheese quesadillas. These are a great app to share for a small group or a light dinner!

FOR THE SUNFLOWER SEED
CREMA

½ cup / 67 g raw sunflower seeds, soaked in water for an hour

1 clove garlic

2 tablespoons extra-virgin olive oil

2 tablespoons lime juice

¼ cup / 60 ml water

1 teaspoon sea salt

Freshly ground pepper

8 small tortillas

1 large baked sweet potato

Mushroom "Carnitas" (page 187)

2 cups / 227 g shredded Mexican cheese

1 bundle of cilantro, chopped

Makes 4 servings

For the crema, drain the soaked sunflower seeds. In a food processor or blender, combine all the crema ingredients. Run until completely smooth, about 1 minute. Set aside.

Heat a large skillet over medium heat. Set up an assembly line: one tortilla, smash in a few spoonfuls of the baked sweet potato, a sprinkle of the mushrooms, some cheese, and some cilantro, and top with another tortilla. Repeat with the remaining tortillas.

Grease the skillet and cook the quesadillas, 2 minutes on each side. Remove from the pan, slice in quarters, and drizzle with a bit of the sunflower crema.

CHANGE IT UP

These are perfect as is, but my people *love* a crispy crust of cheese charred to the outside of the tortilla for a salty crunch. Before you cook the quesadillas, sprinkle a little pile of cheese onto the hot skillet (ideally nonstick or cast iron), then lay the quesadilla right on top. It will brown and stick right to the tortilla, giving you a great frico crust.

MAKE AHEAD

The crema and potatoes can be prepared up to 3 days in advance.

White Bean Bruschetta

I find that adding white beans to a classic bruschetta adds some heft while also helping it stay on the bread. Mashing them adds viscosity to the mixture, and there are enough other bold flavors going on to carry it all perfectly on toast. If you have the grill going, grill the bread and rub the garlic on the crust from there. I tend to use Roma tomatoes, but honestly, any small-ish, fragrant, ripe tomato is great here.

1 (13-ounce / 368 g) can cannellini beans, drained

2 large cloves garlic, grated

2 ounces / 56 g sundried tomatoes, in oil, minced

2 cups chopped ripe Roma tomatoes (about 4)

½ teaspoon dried oregano

¼ teaspoon red pepper flakes, to taste

2 tablespoons extra-virgin olive oil

2 teaspoons white balsamic vinegar

½ teaspoon sea salt, to taste

¼ teaspoon freshly ground pepper

2 ounces / 56 g basil, sliced finely into a chiffonade, divided

1 baguette

1 clove garlic

Extra-virgin olive oil

Flaky salt

Shaved Parmesan, optional

Makes 12 toasts

Preheat the oven to 375°F / 190°C.

Put the beans in a mixing bowl and smash them with the back of a fork. Not smooth, just like a half mash. Add the grated garlic, sundried tomatoes, fresh tomatoes, oregano, red pepper flakes, olive oil, vinegar, and salt and pepper. Stir to mix.

Stir in half of the fresh basil. Set aside.

Slice your baguette into 1-inch / 2.5 cm slices, on a diagonal. Arrange them on a rimmed baking sheet and toast for 5 minutes until barely golden. Pull the baking sheet from the oven and rub the tops of the crostini with the garlic clove, then drizzle lightly with olive oil.

Scoop a heaping spoonful of the bruschetta onto the crostini. Garnish with flaky salt and more fresh basil. Add a shave of fresh Parmesan if you wish.

MAKE AHEAD
The topping can be prepped a day ahead, but stir in the salt and basil just before assembly.

Butternut + Chorizo Flatbread with Pepita Pesto

If you're feeling frisky, start with the Day-Ahead Pizza Dough (page 292) the day before you plan to serve these. But, to be honest, I usually make these on good store-bought naan. If I take them to someone else's house, I assemble the naan on a large rimmed baking sheet and then bake them in a hot oven when I get to said destination.

Look for a dry-cured chorizo, which is more the texture of salami than a ground sausage. I have found it presliced or in a log in the deli section.

1 medium butternut squash, cut into ½-inch / 1 cm cubes (about 3 heaping cups / 420 g)

2 tablespoons extra-virgin olive oil

1 teaspoon paprika

½ teaspoon sea salt

Freshly ground pepper

PEPITA PESTO

2 cloves garlic

1 large bundle cilantro

3 slices of jalapeño

⅓ cup / 40 g roasted pepitas

1 teaspoon sea salt

1 tablespoon lime juice

3 tablespoons / 28 g grated Parmesan cheese

⅓ cup / 80 ml olive oil

Day-Ahead Pizza Dough (page 292) or 4 pieces of naan

¼ of a red onion, thinly sliced

2 ounces / 57 g dry-cured chorizo, thinly sliced

4-ounce / 113 g ball mozzarella cheese or nondairy alternative

Baby arugula, for garnish

Makes 2 large or 4 small pizzas

Preheat the oven to 425°F / 220°C. Put the butternut cubes on a rimmed baking sheet. Drizzle them with the oil, paprika, salt, and pepper and toss to coat. Roast for 20 minutes, stirring halfway through, until tender and golden on the edges. Set aside.

While your squash bakes, make the pesto. In a food processor, combine the garlic, cilantro, and jalapeño and give it a few pulses to break down. Add the pepitas, salt, and lime juice and run the processor. With the motor running, sprinkle in the Parmesan and drizzle in the olive oil. Season to taste and set aside. Both the pesto and the roasted squash can be prepared in advance.

Preheat a cast-iron skillet on the stovetop over medium heat. Roll out the dough and press it to the edges of the skillet. Spread a few spoonfuls of pesto over the top, sprinkle the squash, onion, and chorizo, then tear up the cheese and sprinkle that generously over the top. Alternatively, arrange the naan on a rimmed baking sheet and assemble straight from there.

Pop the skillet or baking sheet in the upper third of the oven and bake the pizza for around 8 minutes, or until the crust and cheese on top turns golden. Remove to cool slightly, top it with baby arugula, slice, and serve. Repeat with the remaining dough and toppings.

CHANGE IT UP

Vegetarian: Simply skip the meat or add some thinly sliced, roasted mushrooms.

Crostini version: Gently toast some crostini. Add the toppings but use a crumble of goat cheese over the top instead of the mozzarella. I've added pomegranate arils here for color too!

Pizza Knots

My Cleo girl's favorite food! I brought these to an after-school park date one afternoon, and the kids' friends still request them—warm and barely cheesy and fragrant with garlic butter.

The knot making here is messy and imperfect. They can be dough tangles and still taste as delicious. We are making the knots with handmade dough and it just looks rustic and I like it. Pizza in the name implies tomato will be a part of things, so I use paste versus sauce to impart less water.

Like most bread items, these are a dream fresh out of the oven. Because my kids like these as an after-school snack, I will prepare a batch through the knotting stage, freeze half before baking, and complete the steps for the other half to eat fresh out of the oven. When you're ready, leave the frozen ones out at room temperature overnight to defrost, and bake them off the following day.

If you want them to be more pizza-y, tuck a nub of mozzarella cheese (or even a pepperoni) in the knot.

1 batch of Day-Ahead Pizza Dough (page 292) or 1 pound / 453 g premade pizza dough, room temperature

4-6 tablespoons / 56-85 g tomato paste

4 tablespoons / 56 g salted butter

2 cloves garlic, grated

⅔ cup / 65 g finely grated Parmesan cheese

2 teaspoons dried Italian seasoning

Pinch of red pepper flakes

Freshly ground pepper

Makes 12 knots

Line a rimmed baking sheet with parchment paper.

Flour a work surface and roll out your pizza dough into two 12-by-6-inch / 30-by-15 cm rectangles. Brush the top with a thin layer of tomato paste. Cut the dough widthwise into 2-inch- / 5 cm-wide "ribbons." Cross the ends, tie a knot, then press the ends together and tuck them in (yes, these will get a little messy, and imperfect is fine!). Arrange the knots on the prepared sheet. Let them rest while you preheat the oven.

Preheat the oven to 425°F / 220°C.

Bake on the middle rack for 12 to 15 minutes, or until the tops are golden.

While the knots bake, warm the butter and grated garlic until just fragrant and melted. In another bowl, combine the Parmesan, Italian seasoning, pepper flakes, and freshly ground pepper.

Right out of the oven, paint the garlic butter on the knots, then roll them in the Parmesan mixture and set them back on the baking sheet. Serve warm.

Halloumi Skewers with Nectarines + Mint Chimichurri

These can be assembled a few hours in advance, so in the hustle of having people over, most of the work is done. The sauce has a welcome kick that pairs perfectly with sweet summer nectarines and creamy halloumi. If you are not a halloumi person, chunks of extra-firm tofu or chicken are great as well; simply double the grilling time. To make an entrée of things, serve over rice and greens.

Be sure to clean your grill grates and oil everything generously to keep the nectarines from sticking. Fun fact: A cast-iron grill pan is an alternative gateway to those grill marks for those who don't have a grill.

I find small appetizer skewers online or at well-stocked cooking stores like Sur La Table for a smaller version.

6-inch / 15 cm skewers, for grilling

8 ounces / 226 g halloumi, cut in 1-inch / 2.5 cm chunks

1 small red onion, cut in 1-inch / 2.5 cm chunks

2 nectarines, pitted and cut in 1-inch / 2.5 cm chunks

3 tablespoons / 45 ml extra-virgin olive oil

1 teaspoon dried oregano

1 teaspoon sea salt

1 teaspoon freshly ground pepper

FOR THE MINT CHIMICHURRI

2 cloves garlic, chopped

1 serrano pepper, seeded

½ teaspoon ground coriander

1 bundle cilantro

½ cup / 10 g fresh mint leaves

2 teaspoons honey

Juice of 1 lime

⅓ cup / 75 ml extra-virgin olive oil

1 teaspoon sea salt, to taste

Makes about 6 large or 10 small skewers

Preheat your grill or grill pan to medium-high heat. Soak your skewers if using wood ones.

Thread chunks of halloumi, onion, and nectarine on the skewers, repeating the pattern one more time. Paint them generously with the olive oil and season with the oregano, salt, and pepper.

Make the chimichurri. In a blender or food processor, pulse the garlic and seeded serrano to chop. Add the coriander, cilantro, mint, honey, lime juice, olive oil, and sea salt and pulse again until roughly chopped—the herbs should be tiny, but the sauce should still have some texture. Set aside.

Grill the skewers for 4 minutes, rotate, and grill another 4 minutes until you have some good grill marks. Transfer the skewers to a platter or baking sheet and brush the mint chimichurri over the top.

Serve these warm or at room temperature.

Grilled Peach + Burrata Salad with Breadcrumb Crispies

I consider this a side dish for a summer backyard BBQ, either as a salad or to pile on grilled bread. It is a simple summer crowd-pleaser when you get your hands on perfect tomatoes and peaches, the ones you can smell just by being near them.

If you have your food processor out, make pesto from scratch (page 280) but a trusted shortcut is the one at Costco. It is pretty great; just add a splash of water and lemon to thin it.

FOR THE CRUMBS

½ a loaf of day-old sourdough or country bread (GF works)

2 tablespoons extra-virgin olive oil

1 teaspoon dried Italian herbs

1 teaspoon garlic powder

½ teaspoon sea salt

½ teaspoon pepper

2 tablespoons grated Parmesan cheese

Extra-virgin olive oil

2 peaches, pitted and cut in thick wedges

FOR THE VINAIGRETTE

¼ cup / 110g prepared pesto (page 280)

1 tablespoon water

2 tablespoons fresh lemon juice

2 cups / 40 g baby arugula

1 bundle of basil, torn

1 pint / 300 g cherry tomatoes, halved

1 tablespoon extra-virgin olive oil

1 tablespoon balsamic vinegar

Sea salt and pepper

2 balls (4 ounces / 113 g) of burrata, drained and split

⅓ cup / 40 g toasted pine nuts

Serves 4

For the breadcrumbs, tear up the bread and pulse in a food processor until you get large pebbly crumbs. Preheat the oven to 375°F / 190°C and dump the crumbs onto a rimmed baking sheet. Drizzle on the oil, sprinkle with the dried Italian herbs, garlic powder, salt, and pepper, and toss to coat. Bake for 10 minutes, stir, sprinkle the grated Parmesan on top, and bake another 5 minutes. Set aside to cool and crisp up.

Heat your grill or grill pan to medium heat. Oil the pan and all sides of the peaches and season with salt and pepper. Grill the peaches, flesh-side down, for about 4 minutes per side. Remove to cool.

Stir together the pesto vinaigrette ingredients.

Toss the arugula, basil, and tomatoes with the olive oil, balsamic, and a big pinch of salt and pepper. Arrange the greens on a serving platter with the peaches on top, and finish with the split burrata balls. Drizzle the pesto vinaigrette, sprinkle with the breadcrumbs and toasted pine nuts, and serve immediately.

MAKE AHEAD
The pesto vinaigrette and breadcrumbs can be made a day in advance.

After-School Banana Chocolate Chip Chunkers

These cookie-meets-muffin nuggets can stand in for breakfast on-the-go or an afternoon snack and are packable in a school lunch. They are tender and moist, so keep them covered and in the fridge if they'll be around for more than two days.

My family prefers them with mini chocolate chips, or I make them with raisins and finely grated carrots if I'm feeling virtuous. This is not like traditional cookie dough; it's a bit looser and works great with a 1-ounce / 30 g / #40 cookie scoop.

1 large extra-ripe banana (¾ cup / 170 g mashed)

1 large egg

4 tablespoons / 60 ml coconut oil, warmed

⅓ cup / 72 g light brown sugar

1 teaspoon vanilla extract

1 teaspoon cinnamon

½ teaspoon salt

1 cup / 96 g almond flour

½ cup / 40 g quick-cooking oats

3 tablespoons / 32 g coconut flour

2 tablespoons flaxseed meal

½ teaspoon baking soda

½ teaspoon baking powder

⅓ cup / 57 g mini chocolate chips, or 3 ounces / 85 g chopped chocolate

Makes 14 servings

In a mixing bowl, smash up the banana into a puree. Add the egg, coconut oil, sugar, vanilla, cinnamon, and salt and mix to combine. Add the almond flour, oats, coconut flour, flaxseed meal, baking soda, and baking powder and stir again to combine. Stir in the chocolate chips.

Chill the mixture for at least 30 minutes.

Preheat the oven to 360°F / 185°C and line a baking sheet with parchment paper. Arrange 2-tablespoon-size lumps with a little space between. Bake on the middle rack for 13 to 15 minutes until the edges are a little toasty. Set aside to cool.

Chunkers will store at room temperature for 2 to 3 days and in the fridge for a week.

CHANGE IT UP
Nut free: An all-purpose or 1:1 gluten-free flour can replace the almond flour if you need them to be nut free.

Blackberry Gin Spritz

Don't skip the blackberry simple syrup. It feels fancy and tastes fresh and beautiful. It also takes all of three minutes and some cool-down time. The syrup keeps for months and is great with some seltzer and lime juice.

Thank you to my brilliant friend Nellie for this combination that I've since adopted as my signature cocktail for dinners with friends.

The recipe also works great with tequila blanco and lime in place of the lemon!

½ cup / 100 g cane sugar

½ cup / 120 ml water

6 ounces / 170 g fresh blackberries

Pinch of salt

Sprig of rosemary

2 sprigs of rosemary

4 ounces / 120 ml gin

2 ounces / 60 ml fresh grapefruit juice

½ ounce / 15 ml fresh lemon juice

Seltzer water

Makes 2 cocktails

In a small saucepan over medium heat, combine the sugar, water, blackberries, pinch of salt, and rosemary. Simmer until the sugar is dissolved, about 3 minutes. Smash up the blackberries. Let the mixture cool down. Strain the syrup into a container. This can be done well in advance.

Fill a cocktail shaker (or large jar) with ice. Fill two small glasses with ice and a sprig of rosemary. To the cocktail shaker, add 3 ounces / 90 ml of the blackberry syrup, the gin, grapefruit juice, and lemon juice and shake everything up well. Strain into two prepared glasses. Top with a splash of seltzer water and give it one more stir. Enjoy immediately!

BATCHED!

This cocktail batches well. To scale this up to serve eight, triple the recipe for the blackberry syrup (you'll be left with a little extra) and multiply the other amounts by four. Keep the cocktail stored in the fridge until ready to serve and let folks splash with seltzer as they serve themselves.

Watermelon Margaritas

Lest I need to say it, these are best in the summer. We need watermelon juice that tastes like watermelon, which can happen by blending and straining a fresh one yourself or purchasing a cold-pressed version in a bottle, typically available in the summer months.

Outside of summer, subbing pineapple juice, which has a longer season, is a great alternative.

Handful of mint leaves + more for garnish

Pinch of salt

3 ounces / 90 ml watermelon juice

2 ounces / 60 ml fresh lime juice

Squeeze of agave nectar

Grind of fresh pepper

5 ounces / 150 ml tequila blanco

Makes 2 cocktails

In the bottom of a cocktail shaker, muddle the mint and salt to release some flavor.

Fill the cocktail shaker and two glasses with ice.

To the cocktail shaker, add the watermelon juice, lime juice, squeeze of agave, black pepper, and tequila. Shake everything very well and strain into your prepared glasses.

Garnish with lime, fresh mint, or a skewer of watermelon cubes.

Beachside Mai Tais

This is the beverage of our family vacations or a beach day in Laguna. They are sweet and rich, as rum cocktails usually are, but there is really nothing like it on a hot, sunny day. Yes, you do need both kinds of rum. We use a little more fresh juice than a classic recipe because it tastes fresh that way. A dash of almond extract has been a quick substitute when we don't have Orgeat—an almond and orange-flower syrup. As it goes with cocktails—actually food and cooking in general—quality liquor and juices matter here. If you can scavenge some cold-pressed or fresh pineapple juice, you will feel like you're in Hawaii.

2 ounces / 60 ml light rum

1½ ounces / 45 ml dark rum
+ more to float

½ ounce / 15 ml Cointreau

2 ounces / 60 ml pineapple juice

1 ounce / 30 ml fresh orange juice

1 ounce / 30 ml fresh lime juice

½ ounce / 30 ml Orgeat

Wedges of pineapple, for garnish

Slices of lime, for garnish

Makes 2 cocktails

Fill a cocktail shaker and two glasses with ice. Add all the ingredients to the shaker and shake well.

Strain the cocktail between the prepared glasses, give one small splash of dark rum on top, and garnish with a wedge of fresh pineapple and slice of lime.

CHAPTER 3

SALADS + SIDES

92 Fattoush with Za'atar Lavash

93 Anywhere Slaw

95 Peach + Lentil Salad with Black Pepper Vinaigrette

96 Summer Panzanella Salad

99 Quinoa Salad with Watermelon + Golden Beets

100 Sesame Cucumber Crunch

103 Curried Carrot Salad

104 Chopped Greens with Sweet Potatoes, Dates,
     Apples + Crispy Shallots

110 Citrus Chicken Salad with Goat Cheese Dressing

113 Sesame Noodle Slaw

117 Arugula + Mapled Squash Salad

118 Jeweled Farro Salad with Caramelized Carrots
     + Pomegranate Seeds

121 Lemon and Parm Broccoli

122 Tahini-Glazed Cauliflower

125 Mexican Caesar Brussels with Cornbread Crispies

126 Holiday Greens

131 Mixed Roasted Potatoes

132 Spicy Street Corn

Fattoush with Za'atar Lavash

This is the quickest of summer salads and is going to call for the best tomatoes you can find. Because I am a sucker for color, I like to mix cherry tomatoes, kumatos, and other delicious summer tomatoes for a variety of color and texture. You don't need to be this high maintenance; any one kind is fine.

Sumac is a Middle Eastern spice that is acidic, kind of lemony, and adds nice flavor to the lavash and dressing. It's easier to find these days, and definitely online if not at your market. The crispy lavash or pita can be made a day in advance, but don't mix it with the vegetables until just ready to serve.

2 lavash wraps or pita breads

2 tablespoons olive oil

½ teaspoon sea salt

2 teaspoons za'atar

1 teaspoon sumac, optional

FOR THE DRESSING

3 tablespoons / 45 ml lemon juice

1 large clove of garlic, grated

¼ cup / 60 ml extra-virgin olive oil

1 teaspoon agave nectar

½ teaspoon sumac

½ teaspoon za'atar

½ teaspoon sea salt

Freshly ground pepper

2 little gem or baby romaine lettuces, chopped

2 radishes, shaved thin

1½ pounds / 680 g assorted small tomatoes

1 English cucumber

½ a small red onion, shaved thin, rinsed

½ cup / 10 g torn flat-leaf parsley

½ cup / 10 g torn mint leaves

4 ounces / 113 g feta cheese, preferably sheep's milk

Serves 4

Preheat the oven to 375°F / 180°C and line a baking sheet with parchment paper. Rip up the lavash or pita into 2-inch / 5 cm pieces and spread them on the baking sheet. Use your hands to rub the olive oil on both sides and spread them so there is minimal overlap. Sprinkle with the sea salt, za'atar, and sumac, if using. Toast the lavash for 4 to 5 minutes, until just golden. Remove to cool.

Put all the dressing ingredients in a jar and shake to mix. Set aside.

Collect the lettuce and radishes in a large, shallow bowl. Chop the tomatoes in halves and quarters, depending on size. Slice the cucumber in half lengthwise and seed it, then dice. Add the tomatoes, cucumber, and shaved onion to the bowl. Drizzle the vegetables with the vinaigrette to taste and toss to coat. Season with salt and pepper as needed, add both herbs, half of both the feta cheese and lavash crisps, and toss again.

Finish the salad with the remaining cheese and lavash crisps. Serve immediately.

CHANGE IT UP

To make this an entrée, roast some marinated chicken, cool, and shred it up to incorporate it into the salad. In this case, double the dressing.

To make this kid friendly, chop all the vegetables small, dress them, and put them in a soft lavash wrap with hummus and shredded chicken. Think Mediterranean burritos.

Anywhere Slaw

We use this slaw as a taco topping or with shredded BBQ chicken in a soft, toasted bun. It can be a lighter side dish that goes with hot dogs at your block party, or what you bring over when your friend is smoking a brisket. A slaw is best when it's crunchy and simple and not overly dressed.

I cannot encourage using a mandoline or shred blade on a food processor enough here. Having all the cabbage thin and evenly sliced makes a big difference to the texture (and beauty) of the slaw. I know rinsing an onion sounds strange, but it prevents the flavor taking over.

½ a red onion, thinly sliced, rinsed

Zest and juice of 2 limes

¼ teaspoon sea salt

Dash of hot sauce

FOR THE DRESSING

2 tablespoons avocado oil

3 tablespoons / 45 ml mayonnaise or Vegenaise

3 tablespoons / 45 ml apple cider vinegar

½ teaspoon Dijon mustard

2 teaspoons cane sugar

½ teaspoon sea salt

Freshly ground pepper

1 small head of green cabbage

½ a small head of purple cabbage

½ a bunch of lacinato kale, de-ribbed and cut into thin ribbons

1 small jalapeño, seeded and thinly sliced

1 bundle cilantro, roughly chopped

½ cup / 60 g toasted, salted pepitas

Serves 6

In a large mixing bowl, combine the onion, lime zest and juice, salt, and hot sauce and stir to mix. Let that all sit for 15 minutes while you prepare the rest.

Mix up your dressing ingredients and set aside.

Halve and core the cabbages and slice them thin. To your onion bowl, add both cabbages, kale ribbons, jalapeño, and dressing and toss to coat. Add the cilantro and pepitas and toss again. Taste for seasoning and serve.

MAKE AHEAD
Cut up all your vegetables and soak your onions in advance. This can sit dressed and stored in the fridge for a few hours, especially if you prefer your cabbage a bit more tender.

Peach + Lentil Salad with Black Pepper Vinaigrette

A meal salad! My favorite, especially in the summer when I want something a bit lighter. Adding quinoa and lentils makes this salad filling, and the spicy, punchy dressing, crunchy seeds, and sweet peaches check all the flavor and texture boxes. If you have a mandoline, use that here for the onions and cucumbers. If you're already going to the trouble of making the dressing, just double it; it goes on all sorts of salads and will last for two weeks in the fridge.

FOR THE DRESSING

2 tablespoons minced shallot

1 tablespoon honey

1 clove garlic, chopped

1 teaspoon Dijon mustard

¼ cup / 15 g toasted pistachios

¼ cup / 60 ml apple cider vinegar

1 tablespoon lemon juice

⅓ cup / 80 ml olive oil

1 tablespoon water

½ teaspoon sea salt

1 teaspoon freshly ground black pepper

Handful of flat-leaf parsley

FOR THE PEPITAS

1 tablespoon unsalted butter

1 tablespoon maple syrup

½ teaspoon sea salt

Pinch of cayenne, optional

⅔ cup / 40 g raw pepitas

FOR THE SALAD

1 head of romaine, thinly sliced

2 cups / 40 g baby arugula

2 Persian cucumbers, thinly sliced

½ of a red onion, thinly sliced, rinsed

¾ cup / 150 g cooked dark green/ Puy lentils

1 cup / 185 g cooked quinoa

2 peaches, pitted and diced

4 ounces / 113 g feta, crumbled

Serves 2-4

For the dressing, combine all the ingredients in a small blender or food processor and run until mostly smooth. Set aside in the fridge until ready to use.

Lay out a piece of parchment paper for cooling the pepitas. In a medium saucepan over medium heat, warm the butter to a liquid. Add the maple syrup, salt, and a pinch of cayenne if you like kick, and stir to warm through. Add the pepitas, stirring occasionally until they start to look toasty and some of the liquid is evaporated, about 3 to 4 minutes. Remove them to the parchment to cool completely. They will crisp up as they cool.

Meanwhile, prepare the salad ingredients. Put the romaine and arugula in a bowl. Add the shaved cucumbers, onion, lentils, quinoa, half of the peaches and feta, and desired amount of dressing. Toss everything to coat. Top with the remaining peaches, feta, and pepitas.

CHANGE IT UP
Dairy free: Simply skip the cheese.

If you need a shortcut, buy toasted, seasoned pumpkin seeds/pepitas, which are available at most markets, and fold them into the warmed butter mixture.

Summer Panzanella Salad

This salad is best plated (or shallow bowled!) so you can scrape up a bit of that pillowy feta sauce with your vegetables. The croutons will stay crunchier the larger they are, but I like how small ones find their way into the tangle of vegetables. It's a great light summer salad, both satisfying and refreshing. Sweet 100 tomatoes are a specific line item here, because they are tiny and have incredible flavor. Yes, any smaller tomato will be fine, but this tomato-focused salad really shines when you work with some great ones.

FOR THE DRESSING

2 tablespoons minced shallot

2 garlic cloves, grated

2 tablespoons fresh lemon juice

3 tablespoons / 45 ml extra-virgin olive oil

1 teaspoon Dijon mustard

½ teaspoon sea salt

¼ teaspoon freshly ground pepper

FOR THE WHIPPED FETA

¾ cup / 168 g plain, whole milk yogurt

4 ounces / 113 g sheep's milk feta cheese

¼ cup / 5 g chopped flat-leaf parsley

Zest of 1 small lemon

1 tablespoon lemon juice

Sea salt and pepper

1 bulb of fennel, trimmed

1 pint / 300 g sweet 100 tomatoes, halved

2 peaches, pitted and diced

2 Persian cucumbers, thinly shaved

2 cups fresh croutons from the Salad Crunchies recipe (page 290)

Handful of roughly chopped flat-leaf parsley + more for garnish

Handful of basil, julienned + more for garnish

Flaky salt, to finish

Serves 4

In a large bowl, mix together the shallot, grated garlic, lemon juice, olive oil, mustard, salt, and pepper. Set aside.

For the whipped feta, in a food processor, combine the yogurt, feta cheese, parsley, lemon zest, lemon juice, and a pinch of salt and pepper. Whiz until smooth, adding more lemon juice or olive oil if the mixture appears too thick to move. Set aside.

Shave the fennel bulb thinly on a mandoline and add to the bowl along with the tomatoes, peaches, and cucumbers. Toss everything to coat in the dressing. Toss the croutons, parsley, and basil in with the vegetables.

To assemble, smear the whipped feta in the bottom of each bowl (or in one large, low, serving bowl). Top with the panzanella and garnish with parsley, basil, and flaky salt.

CHANGE IT UP

Vegan: Forget the feta sauce, and add some crispy chickpeas and torn olives for heft.

To make it more of a meal, add shredded roasted chicken, grilled shrimp, or salmon.

Quinoa Salad with Watermelon + Golden Beets

Filling, colorful, and highly packable for BBQs and picnics—the sort of salad that can travel and not wilt in moments.

I like to cook my quinoa with less liquid to avoid any possible mushiness in the salad. The beets can be baked in the oven or steamed in a pot until tender, about twenty minutes. Either way, just long enough so you can remove the skin and cut them into cubes. You can use red beets, but I prefer the color contrast.

2 medium golden beets

Olive oil, for rubbing

¾ cup / 135 g quinoa, rinsed

1¼ cups / 340 ml vegetable broth

Salt

Freshly ground pepper

FOR THE DRESSING

2 cloves garlic

3 tablespoons / 30 g minced shallots

⅓ cup / 80 ml extra-virgin olive oil

2 teaspoons Dijon mustard

2 teaspoons agave nectar or honey

¼ cup / 60 ml champagne vinegar

Squeeze of fresh lemon juice

Handful of fresh parsley

Handful of fresh chives

1 teaspoon sea salt

½ teaspoon freshly ground pepper

½ of a small watermelon, cut into small cubes (about 4 cups / 600 g)

2 jalapeños, thinly sliced

1 small bundle fresh mint, roughly chopped, divided

3 cups / 60 g baby arugula

⅓ cup / 50 g Marcona almonds or pistachios, roughly chopped

3 ounces / 80 g ricotta salata (or feta cheese), crumbled, optional

Serves 6

Preheat the oven to 400°F / 200°C. Trim the beets, rub them in a light coat of oil, and wrap them in foil. Roast them for 45 to 60 minutes, depending on size, until you can pierce through the center with a knife. Set aside to cool. Peel and dice into 1-inch / 2.5 cm cubes.

While the beets roast, make your quinoa. Put the quinoa and broth or water in a pot along with a big pinch of salt and pepper. Bring to a simmer, cover, and cook for 13 to 15 minutes. Remove the lid, turn off the heat, fluff with a fork, and set it aside to cool with the lid generously ajar. Stir occasionally to let the steam out.

To make the dressing, in a blender or food processor, pulse the garlic and shallots. Add the oil, Dijon, agave, vinegar, lemon juice, herbs, salt and pepper, and pulse again to combine.

In a mixing bowl, toss the beets with a few spoonfuls of the dressing. Add the watermelon, jalapeños, and half of the mint and gently toss again.

Stir a few spoonfuls of the dressing into the cooled quinoa. In a large, shallow serving bowl, toss the quinoa, arugula, and a few more spoonfuls of vinaigrette together. Add the beet and watermelon mixture. Garnish with more mint, salt and pepper, and chopped nuts. Crumble the cheese over the top, if using.

MAKE AHEAD

Beets, quinoa, and dressing can all be made a day in advance.

Sesame Cucumber Crunch

I never know what to pair with teriyaki chicken or the Sesame Seared Ahi Salad Bowls (page 142). The answer: a non-lettuce salad! Everything here gets thinly shredded and tossed with a punchy dressing. This bowl of goodness can be added to a cooked grain and goes with just about any protein. I use a matchstick blade on my mandoline but you could also use the slicer blade attachment on your food processor or a box grater.

FOR THE SALAD

4 cups / 280 g thinly shredded green cabbage

1 cup / 155 g shelled edamame

2 Persian cucumbers, halved and seeded

½ pound / 225 g (about 2 cups) snap peas

½ bunch cilantro, chopped

1 bunch fresh mint leaves

5 green onions, trimmed and chopped

3 tablespoons / 30 g sesame seeds

½ cup / 56 g roasted and salted peanuts, chopped

FOR THE HONEY MISO DRESSING

1 tablespoon honey or agave nectar

3 tablespoons / 67 g smooth peanut butter or tahini

1 teaspoon Dijon mustard

1 tablespoon yellow or white miso paste

2 tablespoons fresh lemon juice

2 tablespoons rice vinegar

⅓ cup / 80 ml avocado oil

1–2 teaspoons gochujang, sriracha, or other chili paste

1 clove of garlic, grated

2 teaspoons grated fresh ginger

1 teaspoons sea salt

Freshly ground black pepper

2 avocados, diced

Serves 4

Collect the cabbage and edamame in a large mixing bowl. Trim and slice the cucumbers and snap peas super thin, on a diagonal, and add them to the bowl along with the cilantro, mint, green onions, sesame seeds, and peanuts.

In a jar, combine the honey, peanut butter, mustard, miso, lemon juice, vinegar, avocado oil, gochujang, grated garlic, ginger, salt, and pepper and shake well to mix. You may need to use the back of a fork to get the miso or nut/seed butter moving.

Dress the salad to taste. Serve the salad with avocado on top.

CHANGE IT UP

This is definitely a light side dish, but if you'd like to stretch it, you could add some cooked and rinsed ramen noodles.

MAKE AHEAD

If you are packing this up for a potluck or to take to dinner at a friend's, shake up the dressing separately, and wait to dice up the avocados until just before serving.

Curried Carrot Salad

My best intention is to avoid eating a bar and crackers for lunch, and I can do that when I stock the fridge with "deli salads" like this. They don't need to be eaten immediately, and they pack some fiber and protein in with a delicious dressing.

FOR THE DRESSING

2-inch / 5 cm nub of fresh ginger, peeled and grated

1 clove garlic, grated

1 tablespoon water

1 tablespoon tahini

¼ teaspoon cayenne

1 teaspoon curry powder

2 teaspoons agave nectar

2 tablespoons rice vinegar

1 tablespoon lime juice

½ teaspoon sea salt

¼ teaspoon freshly ground pepper

¼ cup / 60 ml avocado oil

FOR THE SALAD

½ cup / 85 g golden raisins

2 tablespoons rice vinegar

2 tablespoons warm water

4 medium carrots, grated, shredded, or thinly sliced

2 cups / 180 g thinly grated purple cabbage

¼ of a small red onion

1 (13-ounce / 368 g) can chickpeas, rinsed and drained

1 bundle of cilantro, roughly chopped

1 bunch of fresh mint leaves, roughly chopped

¾ cup / 98 g toasted cashews, roughly chopped

¾ cup / 45 g unsweetened shaved coconut, toasted

Sea salt and pepper, to taste

Serves 4

To make the dressing, combine the ginger, garlic, water, and tahini in a small mixing bowl. Add the cayenne, curry powder, agave, rice vinegar, lime juice, salt, and pepper and mix to combine. Whisk in the oil and set aside.

In a small bowl, combine the raisins, vinegar, and warm water. Stir, then let them sit to hydrate for 10 minutes while you prepare the other ingredients.

Put the grated carrots and cabbage into a large mixing bowl. Mince the red onion and add it, along with the chickpeas, cilantro, and mint. Toss it all with a generous amount of dressing. Drain the raisins and toss those in along with the cashews and toasted coconut. Taste for salt and pepper.

The salad can be kept covered in the fridge for up to 3 days at this point, though you'll lose some crunch as days pass.

CHANGE IT UP

If you want to stretch this, add some cooked and cooled brown rice or quinoa.

MAKE AHEAD

This salad saves well and is easy to pack: just keep the cashews and coconut on the side to add before serving, so they stay crunchy. The herbs will start to wilt after a day, but the flavor will still be there.

Chopped Greens with Sweet Potatoes, Dates, Apples + Crispy Shallots

One of my secrets to salad success is to have a heavy goodies-to-lettuce ratio, and to also make sure said goodies are prepared super small, so the salad is not laborious to eat. A follow-up secret is to consider crunch, something sweet, something spicy, and something fatty so all your taste buds are catered to.

Hugh says his favorite salads can be eaten with a large spoon, and we can check that box here. We make it with sweet potatoes year-round, or squash in the fall. If this is part of a dinner spread, and we don't have picky kids to consider, a thinly sliced jalapeño is a nice addition. You can sub in a bag of coleslaw mix in place of some of the greens for an even more colorful, sturdier, slaw-like vibe!

FOR THE CRISPY SHALLOTS

2 small shallots, peeled and thinly sliced

¼ cup / 60 ml avocado oil

FOR THE SWEET POTATOES

1 large sweet potato, peeled and diced into ½-inch / 1.25 cm cubes

½ teaspoon sea salt

½ teaspoon freshly ground pepper

1 teaspoon chili powder

Salad Crunchies (page 290)

Double Mustard Maple Dressing (page 289)

Preheat the oven to 425°F / 220°C. Line a rimmed baking sheet with parchment paper. Set aside while you make the shallots.

For the crispy shallots, put the sliced shallots and oil in a small, shallow pan. The oil should cover the shallots. Line a plate with paper towels. Turn the heat up to medium and cook until the shallots are golden, moving them around with a fork halfway through so both sides crisp, about 5 to 7 minutes total. You want to start pulling them on the lighter end of golden, as they can turn dark quickly. Remove from the oil and set aside to drain and crisp on the paper towel–lined plate. Reserve the shallot oil for roasting the sweet potatoes and making the croutons.

Place the sweet potatoes on the prepared baking sheet and drizzle over 2 tablespoons of the reserved shallot oil, sea salt, pepper, and chili powder. Toss to coat. Spread them in a single layer and roast for 20 to 25 minutes. Remove to cool completely.

While the potatoes cool, prepare your salad crunchies and dressing. Set the crunchies aside to cool before adding to the salad.

4 cups / 84 g chopped lacinato kale

5 cups / 235 g romaine or baby arugula

½ cup / 100 g cooked black or Puy lentils, optional

1 apple, cut in small cubes

1 small fennel bulb, cored and thinly sliced

5 dates, pitted and diced

1 cup / 20 g torn herbs—cilantro, parsley, mint all work!

4 ounces / 113 g hard goat cheese or Manchego, grated

Serves 4

To assemble, in a large shallow bowl, drizzle the kale with dressing and massage it with your hands to soften the greens, for about a minute. Add the romaine or arugula, lentils, apple, fennel, dates, herbs, half of the cheese, and the roasted potatoes. Drizzle over more dressing and toss to dress.

Top with the salad crunchies to taste, remaining cheese, and crispy shallots.

CHANGE IT UP

I would consider this a hearty side salad or entrée, but a fried egg or grilled protein of choice could fill it out further.

Dairy free: You can skip the cheese with no other changes.

QUESTIONS FOR THE DINNER TABLE

The most uninspiring question to start a conversation around the table goes "How was your day?" Being a mom of elementary-age kids has taught me that asking very specific questions is the only way to get specific answers. Here are a few I've logged that get us all talking with answers that extend beyond "fine."

What did you learn today?

If you could eat all your favorite things in a day, what would you eat for breakfast, lunch, and dinner?

What did you learn about one of your friends today?

Can you think of a moment today where someone showed generosity to you? What about you toward others?

What do you want to be known for? What do you think you are known for now?

Tell me about your dream birthday party—money and logistics aren't a concern.

What is the best way for people to show you they love you?

In one word, give one affirmation to each person sitting at the table.

What was your peach and pit (high and low) today?

What makes you unique?

I know you want to be a X, Y, Z when you grow up. What would make you good at that job?

Where would you like to go on vacation? What intrigues you about that place?

What was a mistake you made today? What would you do differently next time?

Citrus Chicken Salad with Goat Cheese Dressing

A crowd favorite from SK Cooking Club, this salad is beloved for both its make-ahead options and because it really does shine in the winter months when citrus is best, an otherwise dreary produce season. The chicken benefits from marinating overnight (though it can be done in less time if you're in a rush), and the dressing can sit for up to a week. If you'd prefer a side salad, just omit the chicken.

I blend half of the goat cheese into the dressing, so the creaminess marries with the punchy citrus and crunchy greens.

FOR THE SPICE BLEND

1 teaspoon sea salt

½ teaspoon black pepper

1½ teaspoons paprika

1 teaspoon dried thyme

1 teaspoon garlic powder

Pinch of cayenne

1½ pounds / 680 g chicken breasts, pounded ½ inch / 1.25 cm thin

1 tablespoon avocado oil

FOR THE DRESSING

5 ounces / 140 g goat cheese, divided

4 tablespoons / 60 ml extra-virgin olive oil

1 large clove garlic, grated

1 teaspoon orange zest

3 tablespoons / 45 ml orange juice

3 tablespoons / 45 ml lemon juice

1 teaspoon lemon zest

1 tablespoon champagne vinegar

2 teaspoons honey

Pinch of dried Italian seasoning

½ teaspoon sea salt

Freshly ground pepper

Combine all the spices. Cut the chicken into small 1-inch / 2.5 cm cubes and put them, the oil, and the spice blend in a bowl or bag and toss it around. Let it marinate for at least 20 minutes, ideally overnight in the fridge.

To make the dressing, in a jar and using an immersion blender, or in a blender or food processor, combine half of the goat cheese, the oil, garlic, orange juice and zest, lemon juice and zest, vinegar, honey, Italian seasoning, salt, and pepper. Blend until smooth and creamy. Set aside until ready to use.

CONTINUED

Citrus Chicken Salad with Goat Cheese Dressing, continued

1 small lemon

1 fennel bulb, cored and thinly shaved

1 bunch lacinato kale, de-ribbed and julienned

4 cups / 80 g baby arugula

1 shallot, peeled and thinly sliced

1 cup / 20 g fresh herbs (dill, parsley, basil), roughly chopped

1 medium pink grapefruit, segmented

1 orange, segmented

½ cup / 60 g toasted pistachios, roughly chopped

1 large avocado, cubed

Serves 4

Heat a large skillet over medium-high heat with a thin slick of oil. Carefully add the chicken and sear for about 4 minutes. Shake the pan to prevent the chicken sticking, then cook for 4 to 5 minutes more until cooked through, shaking the pan occasionally. Remove from the heat. Squeeze lemon juice over the top and tent it with foil while you assemble the rest of your salad.

In your salad bowl, combine the shaved fennel, kale, arugula, shallots, and herbs. Add a few spoonfuls of dressing and toss to coat. Add half of the citrus segments and toss again.

To serve, top the greens with chicken, the remaining citrus, remaining goat cheese crumbles, pistachios, and avocado. Serve immediately.

CHANGE IT UP

Dairy free: Sub in a few spoonfuls of vegan mayo in the dressing and skip the cheese.

Vegetarian: And if you're looking to make this vegetarian, this seasoning blend would be great on cubes of tofu and roasted at 425°F / 220°C for 25 minutes to crisp up.

Sesame Noodle Slaw

Don't be deterred by a bit of chopping on the front end; this is an excellent noodle salad with all the crunch and texture. I like my noodle salads heavy on the vegetables, so add another block of ramen noodles if you want yours more noodle-y. It's a meal with the tofu or, if you prefer, chicken or salmon, and a go-to packable lunch. The coconut aminos, a slightly sweet, savory sauce, and chili paste will be at most markets near the soy sauce and similar condiments. Hate cilantro? Use some Thai basil instead. Not a tahini person? Smooth peanut butter is delicious here. It's flexible!

The salad can sit for a day with the vegetables retaining their crunch, making it a great dish to deliver to friends with a new baby or any other big life event.

FOR THE TOFU

14 ounces / 400 g firm tofu, pressed of extra liquid

1 tablespoon tamari or soy sauce

2 tablespoons coconut aminos

2 teaspoons chili paste (I like sambal oelek, but gochujang and chili crisp are fine too)

1 tablespoon toasted sesame oil

FOR THE DRESSING

2 tablespoons toasted sesame oil

1 tablespoon avocado oil

3 tablespoons / 45 ml tahini

1 tablespoon white or yellow miso

3 tablespoons / 45 ml lime juice

2 tablespoons rice vinegar

2 cloves of garlic, grated

3-inch / 7.5 cm nub of ginger, grated

1 tablespoon agave nectar

2 teaspoons chili paste

Freshly ground pepper

8 ounces / 225 g ramen noodles

Preheat the oven to 425°F / 220°C and line a baking sheet with parchment paper. Drain the tofu and press it between dishcloths or layers of paper towels to dry. Cut it into small cubes. In a mixing bowl, combine the tamari, coconut aminos, chili paste, and sesame oil and add the tofu to coat. This can be done in advance and left to marinate overnight. Spread the tofu on the baking sheet and roast for 25 minutes, stirring halfway through. Set aside.

Meanwhile, make the dressing. In a jar, shake up all the dressing ingredients until smooth and combined. It may need a splash of water if things seize up. Shake again.

Cook the noodles according to package instructions. Drain, then rinse with cold water.

CONTINUED

Sesame Noodle Slaw, continued

1 bell pepper, julienned

1 carrot, julienned

2 packed cups / 150 g shaved savoy cabbage

2 packed cups / 150 g shaved purple cabbage

1 bunch of cilantro, roughly chopped

½ cup / 5 g mint leaves, torn

¼ of a red onion, thinly shaved

¼ cup / 35 g toasted sesame seeds, divided

½ cup / 60 g unsweetened coconut flakes, toasted

2 avocados, peeled and diced

Serves 4–6

In a large mixing bowl, combine the noodles, bell pepper, carrots, cabbages, cilantro, mint, red onion, and half of the sesame seeds, and toss with your desired amount of dressing. Season to taste. Garnish with the coconut, avocados, tofu, and remaining sesame seeds.

TIP
To keep the noodles from clumping, make sure you're cooking them in a large pot with lots of water and space to cook. Don't overcook them, and rinse them immediately after draining to stop the cooking. Anything from soba, to rice-based noodles, to capellini pasta would be fine substitutes for the ramen.

MAKE AHEAD
Marinate the tofu, shake up your dressing, and chop all the vegetables the day before. You can also substitute two bags of prepared coleslaw mix in place of the cabbages and carrots.

Arugula + Mapled Squash Salad

I bring this salad to our neighborhood friends-giving, which is a traditional meal desperate for color and acidity, if you ask me. The recipe is easily doubled or, with the addition of a protein, turned into an entrée. We've tried it with seared salmon, crispy chicken, or bacon, to great acclaim. The two types of squash not only look pretty but also give some variety in texture. If you want even more, try adding ribboned kale to the arugula for sturdiness.

2 delicata squash (about 1¼ pounds / 570 g)

1 medium butternut squash (1¼ pounds / 570 g)

2–3 tablespoons extra-virgin olive oil or avocado oil

2 tablespoons maple syrup

2 teaspoons paprika

Pinch of cayenne

½ teaspoon sea salt

¼ teaspoon freshly ground pepper

1 tablespoon ghee or coconut oil

⅔ cup / 90 g pepitas

3 tablespoons / 40 g cane sugar

¼ teaspoon sea salt

Pinch of cayenne

1 tablespoon finely chopped rosemary

2 teaspoons Dijon mustard

1 tablespoon maple syrup

3 tablespoons / 45 ml apple cider vinegar

¼ teaspoon sea salt

Freshly ground pepper

¼ cup / 60 ml extra-virgin olive oil

4 cups / 80 g baby arugula

½ of a small red onion, shaved paper thin, rinsed and drained

Feta cheese, optional

Serves 4–6

Preheat the oven to 425°F / 220°C. Line a rimmed baking sheet with parchment paper.

Cut the delicatas in half lengthwise, seed them, and slice into 1-inch / 2.5 cm half-moons. Peel the butternut, halve lengthwise, seed it, and slice it into ½-inch / 1.25 cm half-moons. Pile the squash onto a rimmed baking sheet, drizzle with the olive oil, maple syrup, paprika, cayenne, and salt and pepper. Toss to coat and spread in an even layer (use a second sheet if it looks overcrowded). Roast for 25 minutes, flipping them halfway through, until the edges of the squash are caramelized. Remove to cool to room temperature. This can be done a few hours in advance and left at room temperature.

While the squash roasts, prepare the pepitas. In a saucepan, heat the ghee or coconut oil and toast the pepitas for a couple of minutes. Remove them from the pan. Add the sugar, salt, and cayenne and let the sugar just begin to melt. Add the pepitas back in and sauté until the pan looks mostly dry, about 2 minutes. Stir in the rosemary and then transfer them to a piece of parchment paper to cool completely.

For the dressing, shake in a jar or whisk together the mustard, maple syrup, apple cider vinegar, salt, pepper, and olive oil.

In a large bowl, dress the arugula and onion. Add the squash and toss again. Transfer to a shallow bowl or platter and top with the candied pepitas and cheese, if using.

Jeweled Farro Salad with Caramelized Carrots + Pomegranate Seeds

A lunch salad, a potluck offering, a base for a roasted chicken dinner. It is colorful and textured and great at room temperature, warm, or even cold. Farro typically takes about thirty minutes to cook through, but Trader Joe's and other retailers sell a quick-cooking or pearled option that cooks in a third of the time. You can also cut the time by soaking it in water overnight. If you do not stock sumac, more paprika will be fine here.

1 cup farro

6 medium carrots, a mix of colors, scrubbed clean

3 tablespoons / 35 ml extra-virgin olive oil

1 teaspoon sea salt

½ teaspoon freshly ground pepper

1 teaspoon sumac

1 teaspoon paprika

⅓ cup / 50 g dried fruit, chopped (golden raisins, cherries, cranberries, all great)

Zest and juice of 1 lemon

2 teaspoons Dijon mustard

1 large clove garlic, grated

¼ cup / 60 ml extra-virgin olive oil

½ teaspoon sea salt

3 tablespoons / 45 ml apple cider vinegar

1 bunch rainbow chard (or kale), de-ribbed and sliced into ribbons

4 green onions, white and light green parts thinly sliced

½ cup / 10 g chopped flat-leaf parsley

½ cup / 10 g chopped fresh dill

⅓ cup / 40 g toasted, salted pistachios, chopped

1 cup / 225 g pomegranate seeds

4 ounces / 113 g feta cheese

Serves 4–6

Preheat the oven to 400°F / 200°C.

Rinse and drain the farro. Put the farro in a pot and cover it generously with water. Season with salt. Bring it to a boil and cook, cover ajar, for 25 to 30 minutes (or according to package instructions). Drain and set aside to cool.

While the farro cooks, cut the carrots into ½-inch / 1.25 cm coins, on a diagonal. Put the carrots on a baking sheet. Drizzle them with the oil, salt, pepper, sumac, and paprika and toss to coat. Spread them in an even layer and roast for 25 minutes until golden and just tender. Set aside.

In a salad bowl, combine the dried fruit, lemon zest, and lemon juice. Let the fruit hydrate for a few minutes. Add the Dijon, grated garlic, olive oil, salt, and vinegar and mix to combine. Add the greens and give it all a massage to soften the greens. Add the green onions, parsley, dill, roasted carrots, and drained farro and toss everything to mix. Add half of the pistachios, pomegranate seeds, and feta cheese and toss. Taste for seasoning. Garnish with the remaining pistachios, pomegranate seeds, and cheese and serve.

CHANGE IT UP

Gluten free: Use quinoa and mind your cooking times.

Dairy free: Replace the cheese with torn green olives or just leave it off with no other changes.

MAKE AHEAD

You can make this a day in advance (it really is a good one for that); just save the nuts and cheese until serving.

Lemon and Parm Broccoli

There are hundreds of roasted broccoli recipes, and at a glance, this recipe reads as underwhelming, but it is so good I would be remiss to not include it in a book I hope my kids refer back to as our "house favorites." Seasoning it both before and after it's roasted is key to ensure the fresh citrus still pops and we get the depth of roasted garlic and the kick from fresh. You could incorporate some cooked white beans to make it a more filling side dish. My kids love boxed mac 'n' cheese, and this is what I mix into their shells and white cheddar for my own ego, ahem, I mean their health.

The queen, Ina Garten, led us down this road of roasting broccoli. She always knows her way around simple and delicious.

2½ pounds / 1.1 kg broccoli crowns (about 5 cups florets)

4 cloves garlic, divided

5 tablespoons / 75 ml extra-virgin olive oil, divided

1 teaspoon sea salt, divided

½ teaspoon freshly ground pepper, divided

Zest of 1 small lemon

2 tablespoons lemon juice

½ teaspoon red pepper flakes

¼–⅓ cup / 25–30 g grated Parmesan cheese + more for garnish

¼ cup / 35 g toasted pine nuts

1½ cups / 30 g baby arugula

½ cup / 10 g basil leaves, julienned

Serves 4–6

Preheat the oven to 425°F / 220°C.

Cut the broccoli crowns into small florets, cutting through larger pieces and leaving on just a bit of their stem. Collect them all on a rimmed baking sheet. Smash two of the garlic cloves and add them too. Drizzle it all generously with 3 tablespoons / 45 ml of olive oil, and half of the salt and pepper. Toss to coat. Every floret should be coated in oil, so use more if needed. Spread them in an even layer.

Roast the broccoli for 20 minutes, stirring halfway through, until the edges are just browned.

In a large, shallow mixing bowl, add the remaining 2 tablespoons of oil, grate in the remaining garlic cloves, and add the remaining salt and pepper, the lemon zest and juice, and pepper flakes and stir it together. Add the roasted broccoli to the bowl and give it a toss. Add the Parm, pine nuts, and arugula and toss again. Top it with the fresh basil, another sprinkle of Parm, and serve.

Tahini-Glazed Cauliflower

One of my favorite meals is something I call a Mediterranean bowl bar. I make rice, a generously spiced shawarma chicken, Smoky Eggplant Dip (page 58), Fattoush (page 92), some naan, and this cauliflower. It's tossed with a thin tahini glaze post roast and the dates and mint make it special. It's a standout side for sure. We make roasted cauliflower all the time because it can take on any spice blend, and our kids like it—taco cauliflower, BBQ spiced cauliflower, Italian cauliflower—you get the picture, but this one is my favorite!

1 large head of cauliflower (about 3 pounds / 1.4 kg)

4 tablespoons / 60 g avocado or extra-virgin olive oil

1 teaspoon ground coriander

1 teaspoon ground cumin

½ teaspoon red pepper flakes

1 teaspoon sea salt

½ teaspoon freshly ground pepper

¼ of a small red onion, sliced into thin half-moons

4 ounces / 113 g Medjool dates, pitted and torn into small pieces (about 7 dates)

2 tablespoons white wine vinegar

2 tablespoons tahini

1 tablespoon honey

⅓ cup / 7 g roughly chopped flat-leaf parsley

Handful of baby arugula

½ cup / 10 g mint leaves, divided

¼ cup / 30 g toasted pine nuts

3 tablespoons / 30 g toasted sesame seeds

Serves 4

Preheat the oven to 400°F / 200°C.

Cut the cauliflower florets away from the core and tear them into smaller, quarter-sized pieces. Collect them on a rimmed baking sheet. In a small bowl, whisk together the oil, coriander, cumin, pepper flakes, salt, and pepper. Pour it on the cauliflower and toss to coat, adding more oil if needed to be sure all the cauliflower is coated. Spread the cauliflower in an even layer and roast it for 20 minutes.

Add the onions and dates to the baking sheet and toss them in together with the cauliflower and roast for another 15 to 20 minutes, until the cauliflower is browned on the edges.

In a large mixing bowl, combine the vinegar, tahini, and honey along with 3 tablespoons / 45 ml of water and mix to combine. Add the warm cauliflower mixture and chopped parsley and toss to coat. Season to taste with more salt and pepper. Add the arugula and half of the mint and toss again.

Garnish with the remaining fresh mint, pine nuts, and sesame seeds. Serve warmish or at room temperature.

Mexican Caesar Brussels with Cornbread Crispies

One of our favorite date night spots used to be a (now closed) restaurant in Santa Ana called Playground. The spot was funky and unique, and the menu was always so creative. This is my attempt to knock off one of my favorite items on their menu, a warm salad that hits all the notes: crunchy, spicy, creamy, and sweet.

The recipe calls for prepared cornbread. To save time, I suggest purchasing a premade cornbread in the bakery section of your grocery store. Alternatively, this is a great use for cornbread that's on its way to going stale. You'll need about one-third of a 9-inch / 23 cm pan for this recipe.

Serve these with a protein on the side—roasted chicken, grilled flank steak—or as part of a holiday spread. I don't love to call for two condiments, but! If you have pickled red onions (page 289), those would be great here too.

2 cups / 200 g cornbread

1½ pounds / 680 g Brussels sprouts

2 tablespoons avocado oil

1 tablespoon white wine vinegar

½ teaspoon sea salt

4 green onions, roughly chopped

Mexican Caesar dressing (page 280)

1 bundle of cilantro, roughly chopped, divided

½ cup / 60 g toasted, salted pepitas, divided

½ cup / 60 g crumbled cotija cheese, optional

Serves 4

Preheat the oven to 375°F / 190°C. Line a large, rimmed baking sheet with parchment paper. Break up the cornbread into crumbles, similar in size to a small crouton, and spread them in an even layer. Bake for 15 to 20 minutes, stirring halfway through, until toasted. Set aside.

Turn the oven up to 425°F / 220°C. Trim the ends off your Brussels, and halve or quarter them, depending on size. Add the Brussels to the same prepared baking sheet, along with the oil, vinegar, and salt. Toss to coat and arrange them cut-side down. Roast on the middle rack of the oven for 20 to 25 minutes until browned on the edges. Stir in the green onions and roast another 3 minutes.

Out of the oven, add a few heaping spoonfuls of the dressing onto the sheet, along with half of the cilantro and half of the pepitas, and toss to coat. Transfer everything to a serving dish and top with the remaining cilantro, pepitas, cotija (if using), and cornbread toasty bits.

MAKE AHEAD
The dressing can be made a few days in advance.

Holiday Greens

It took me years to figure this out, even though I've been responsible for bringing the green salad to nearly every family holiday dinner for the last decade. A tender-leafed salad takes up too much room on the plate when sharing real estate with eight other dishes in a buffet. It's laborious to eat and doesn't fare well next to other hot, generally mushy foods. The answer? Slaw-ish things! Or a well-chopped salad, but let's focus on the former. It is easy to get a forkful of this dish, and it gets along well with the other foods it may touch. It is also excellent to prep ahead.

Don't limit yourself by the recipe title. It's great all fall and winter. When pomegranates are no longer available, sub in a shaved green apple or dried cherries. The recipe makes a large salad but is easily doubled for a group. Need it to travel? Prepare all the vegetables together, leave the nuts, cheese, and dressing on the side, and assemble at your destination.

2 bunches Tuscan kale,
ribs removed

1 pound / 450 g Brussels sprouts

1 small fennel bulb, halved
and cored

½ a small red onion, minced
and rinsed

Shallot Date Vinaigrette
(page 283)

¾ cup / 85 g almonds, chopped
and toasted, divided

⅔ cup / 75 g grated Manchego
cheese, divided

1 cup / 190 g pomegranate seeds,
divided

Serves 6

Chiffonade the kale and put it in a large mixing bowl. Use a mandoline on a fairly thin setting or a sharp knife and shave the Brussels sprouts (discarding the ends) and fennel. Add them to the mixing bowl along with the onion.

Dress the salad as you wish, but I suggest using your hands so you can massage it into the kale and Brussels, which tenderizes them a bit. Add half of the almonds, Manchego, and pomegranate seeds and toss again to mix.

Garnish with the remaining almonds, Manchego, and pomegranate seeds and serve.

Mixed Roasted Potatoes

The par boil of the baby Yukons gives these spuds a chance to have the same cooking time as the sweet potatoes, while also giving a great texture to the finished dish. Our favorite balance is 2:1 baby Yukons to sweet potatoes here. This gives you lots of crispy corners mixed with the tenderness of the sweet potatoes.

This mix started because I have one kid who prefers white potatoes and another, orange, and I think this solution consequently makes for a pretty side that goes with just about anything.

1½ pounds / 680 g baby Yukon potatoes

1 pound / 450 g sweet potatoes (1 extra large), peeled

4 cloves garlic, in peel

4 tablespoons / 60 ml avocado or olive oil

2 teaspoons garlic powder

1 teaspoon paprika

½ teaspoon freshly ground pepper

Sea salt

2 tablespoons fresh rosemary, chopped

3 tablespoons / 25 g grated Parmesan cheese, optional

Zest of 1 small lemon

½ cup / 10 g chopped flat-leaf parsley

⅓ cup / 10 g fresh chopped dill

Serves 4–6

Halve the baby potatoes, quartering any of the larger ones. In a large pot, cover the potatoes with water and a few big pinches of salt. Bring the water to a boil and cook for 10 minutes until you can pierce through to the center. Drain the potatoes completely, shake them around to rough up the outsides a bit, and set aside to cool to the touch. Cut the sweet potato into 2-inch / 5 cm chunks.

Preheat the oven to 425°F / 220°C. Collect all the potatoes on a rimmed baking sheet along with the garlic cloves and add the oil, garlic powder, paprika, pepper, and sea salt. Toss everything well to coat and spread them in an even layer on the baking sheet, cut-side down where possible. Bake them in the upper third of the oven for 25 to 30 minutes, add the rosemary, give them a stir, and roast another 5 to 10 minutes until the edges are golden.

Out of the oven, sprinkle with the Parm, a little more salt, lemon zest, parsley, and dill and toss everything together. Serve warm.

CHANGE IT UP

Vegan/Dairy Free: The Parm suggestion gives these a salty boost but doesn't make them "cheesy" per se. You can absolutely skip it if preferred.

Spicy Street Corn

Your taco party needs a side dish, and these *esquites*—a Mexican corn salad—are a little lighter than a traditional version and easy to serve straight from the skillet. I leave the seeds in the jalapeño for some heat, but if you are sensitive to it or feeding kids, remove them. We love the crunch of fresh corn, but frozen (never canned!) corn can work in a pinch.

I like to make this in a large cast-iron pan and serve it straight from the pan with some fish tacos and Hugh's Guacamole (page 57). If you end up with leftovers to reheat, do so over low heat so the dairy doesn't separate.

There are great brands like Love Corn and Trader Joe's making "cleaner versions" of a Corn Nut, the toasted corn listed below. We love those on top for more texture.

2 tablespoons unsalted butter or ghee

1 jalapeño, minced

½ of a white onion, minced

½ teaspoon sea salt

5 ears of corn, husked and cut from the cob, about 3 cups / 435 g

¼ cup / 56 g mayonnaise or Vegenaise

⅓ cup / 75 g sour cream

1 teaspoon chili powder

¼ teaspoon cumin

Pinch of cayenne

Juice of 1 lime

Chopped cilantro

Queso fresco

Toasted corn or pepitas

Serves 4

In a large skillet, heat the butter over medium heat. Add the jalapeño, onion, and salt and sauté for about 3 minutes until the raw edge is just taken off. Stir in the corn and sauté another 4 minutes.

Take the skillet off the heat, add the mayonnaise, sour cream, chili powder, cumin, cayenne, and lime juice and stir again to warm through.

Transfer to your serving dish and garnish with cilantro, queso fresco, and toasted corn. Serve immediately.

CHAPTER 4

A MAIN DISH

138   Blackened Salmon with Tropical Pico

141   Green Harissa Salmon Skewers with Savory Peach + Cucumber Salad

142   Sesame Seared Ahi Salad Bowls

147   Shrimp + Pineapple Sheet Pan Tacos

148   Chicken Milanese with Asparagus + Gribiche Salad

152   Chicken Parmesan Meatballs

157   There's Always Chicken

158   Italian Turkey Burgers with Frico Crisps

163   Harissa Lamb Meatballs with Couscous

165   French Bread Pizzas

168   Spring Spaghetti with Asparagus + Peas

171   THE Veggie Burger with Roasted Tomatoes + Quick Pickles

173   Pasta with Roasted Cauliflower, Chorizo + Winter Pesto

175   Taco Salad with Roasted Jalapeño Ranch

178   Tofu + Mushroom Lettuce Wraps

181   Cauliflower Al Pastor Bowls

182   Roasted Eggplant Rollups

187   Mushroom "Carnitas"

188   Butternut Steaks with Green Apple Relish

191   Winter Bowls with Green Tahini

Blackened Salmon with Tropical Pico

This is your salmon for a crowd, generously seasoned and served with some punchy pineapple pico and avocado. I serve it with coconut rice, but it could just as easily be wrapped into a burrito or even served over greens. This dish makes for excellent lunch leftovers, so don't overthink the suggested serving number.

Salmon season is roughly in the May–September range, and this is when you would be able to find a fresh slab. You can use frozen pieces if that is what is available; just don't use those thin, flimsy tail-end pieces. If you'd prefer not to make the blackened seasoning from scratch, there are many brands that make a blackened blend.

2 tablespoons olive oil + more for the pan

2 pounds / 900 g center-cut slab of salmon

FOR THE BLACKENED SEASONING

1 teaspoon paprika

1 teaspoon onion powder

1 teaspoon garlic powder

½ teaspoon dried thyme

½ teaspoon dried oregano

Pinch of cayenne pepper

1 teaspoon sea salt

1 tablespoon light brown sugar

1 teaspoon finely ground coffee

½ teaspoon freshly ground pepper

FOR THE COCONUT RICE

1 cup / 200 g short-grain white rice, well rinsed

1 cup / 240 ml water

1 cup / 240 ml coconut milk

Pinch of sugar

Zest of 1 lime

Sea salt

2 large avocados, cubed

Tropical Pico (page 62)

Fresh cilantro and microgreens

Serves 4–6

Preheat the oven to 300°F / 150°C. Line a rimmed baking sheet with parchment paper. Spray or rub it with oil. Dry the salmon with a paper towel and place it on the oiled parchment sheet.

Mix all the blackened seasoning ingredients together. Mix in the oil and gently rub it all over the flesh of the salmon.

Start the rice. Combine the rinsed rice, water, coconut milk, sugar, lime zest, and salt together. Stir to mix. Bring the rice to a boil, then down to a simmer. Cover and cook for 18 to 20 minutes until cooked and tender. Set aside.

While the rice cooks, roast the salmon. Bake for 15 minutes, then turn the heat up to broil and cook another few minutes until the top starts to char. Timing will vary by oven, but assume somewhere in the 2-minute ballpark. The salmon should be cooked to about medium in that time; add 5 minutes to that first bake if you prefer it well done. Remove to rest.

Serve the slab of salmon over the rice on a platter, flaking it apart with a fork, with the avocado and pico over the top. Garnish with cilantro and microgreens.

Green Harissa Salmon Skewers with Savory Peach + Cucumber Salad

My recipe for homemade green harissa is bold, well spiced, and perfect to use straight off the grill here. To save time, you can use a store-bought harissa or zhoug with similar results, but sauce is imperative.

Cutting salmon away from the skin at home is tough. Ask the fishmonger or butcher to take off the skin, and you can then cube it at home with a sharp knife. "Center cut" or "BBQ cut" salmon will help you get larger cubes for the skewers, but I know a lot of us buy frozen fish for the sake of availability. Try to avoid thin tail pieces so you have enough width in the fish to skewer.

This dish can come off pretty light, so depending on your audience, add some rice or Mixed Roasted Potatoes (page 131) and you've got yourself a meal for company.

1½ pounds / 680 g boneless, skinless salmon, ideally center cut into 2-inch / 5 cm cubes

Sea salt

6–8 skewers

⅓ cup / 80 ml Green Harissa (page 281)

1 tablespoon honey

1 tablespoon avocado oil

2 peaches

3 Persian cucumbers

½ packed cup / 50 g chopped cilantro + more for garnish

¼ packed cup / 25 g chopped mint + more for garnish

2 tablespoons extra-virgin olive oil

Juice of 1 lime

Flaky sea salt

Freshly ground pepper

2 teaspoons coriander seeds

2 tablespoons toasted sesame seeds

¼ cup / 30 g toasted pepitas

2 avocados

Serves 4

Season the salmon with salt. If you are using wooden skewers, soak them in water to prevent burning.

Combine the harissa, honey, and avocado oil in a mixing bowl and use half to coat the salmon chunks, reserving the rest. Set aside for 15 minutes.

For the salad, pit and slice the peaches, thinly slice the cucumbers into coins, and put them in a mixing bowl with the chopped cilantro, mint, olive oil, lime juice, and a few big pinches of salt and pepper. Toss everything to mix. Crush up the coriander, sesame, and pepitas with a mortar and pestle (or run a knife through them) to get them into smaller pieces and release some of the oil and fragrance. Sprinkle them over the salad. Cut the avocados into large chunks and add them to the bowl, give the salad one more stir, and adjust the seasoning to taste.

Preheat an oiled grill or grill pan to medium-high heat. Thread the fish onto 6–8 skewers. Cook for 4 minutes on each side, just enough to get a char. To broil in the oven, line up the skewers on an oiled rimmed baking sheet and broil on the middle rack for 5 minutes, rotating halfway—we want brown edges but a tender center. Brush on the remaining harissa marinade straight off the heat.

Assemble plates with the salad, salmon skewers, and a garnish of herbs.

Sesame Seared Ahi Salad Bowls

Shopping for fresh fish is tricky. So tricky, that I plan my meal after I find a good-looking piece at the farmers' market or, if I'm lucky, am gifted a fresh piece from the fishermen friends in our life. Fishmongers will point you toward what is freshest, so ask! We want a piece of ahi that is pink or deep red, never brown, and looking moist and shiny. If it smells like, well, old fish, find a different source.

FOR THE COCONUT RICE

1 cup / 200 g short-grain white rice, rinsed well and drained

1 cup / 240 ml water

1 cup / 240 ml coconut milk

Pinch of sugar

Pinch of salt

Zest of 1 lime

FOR THE AHI

1 teaspoon sea salt

1 teaspoon freshly ground pepper

4 tablespoons / 35 g sesame seeds, white and/or black

Avocado or coconut oil, for cooking

1½ pounds / 680 g sushi-grade ahi, steaks or loins

Sesame Cucumber Crunch salad (page 100)

½ cup / 113 g mayonnaise

2 tablespoons sriracha, to taste

Juice of half a lime

2 ripe avocados, sliced

2 watermelon radishes, shaved thin or julienned

1 lime, cut into wedges or rounds

Dried seaweed

Tamari

Pickled ginger, optional

Chili crisp

Serves 4

Put the rinsed and drained rice in a pot with the water and coconut milk. Add a big pinch of sugar, salt, and the lime zest and give it a stir. Bring the rice to a boil, then down to a simmer. Cover and cook for 18 to 20 minutes until cooked and tender. Set aside.

In a wide shallow bowl, stir together the salt, pepper, and sesame seeds. Over medium heat, warm a generous slick of oil in a large pan. Dredge both sides of the ahi in the seed mixture, pressing it into the flesh, then sear the ahi, about 1 minute per side depending on thickness. You are just looking to cook the outside, leaving the inside raw. Remove and set aside on a cutting board.

Prepare your salad. Set aside.

In a small bowl, stir together the mayonnaise, sriracha, and lime juice.

Working against the grain, slice the ahi into ½-inch / 1.25 cm slices.

Assemble bowls with a scoop of rice, a portion of salad, ahi, avocado, radishes, fresh lime, and a generous drizzle of sriracha-mayo sauce. Garnish with dried seaweed.

Serve with tamari, pickled ginger, chili crisp, and more sriracha mayo on the side.

Shrimp + Pineapple Sheet Pan Tacos

This is the quickest weeknight dinner! That is especially true if your sauce and slaw are prepped ahead. To be honest, shrimp is not my favorite, but my field research shows that many folks find it easy to cook at home and it roasts quickly, so here we are. The red Argentinian shrimp from Costco or Trader Joe's have an almost lobster-like texture, so if you too are "eh" about shrimp, try those. Either way, we need them thawed and dried before using them in this recipe.

Yes, there are jalapeños here, but you can remove the seeds to make it more kid friendly, or even sub in mini bell peppers to bring the heat level down.

Below is a small batch of taco seasoning that will make a bit more than you need for this recipe—multiply it by two or three to make a jar to have on hand!

FOR THE TACO SEASONING

1 tablespoon cumin

2 tablespoons chili powder

1 teaspoon coriander

2 teaspoons sea salt

1 teaspoon brown sugar

1 teaspoon paprika

Pinch of pepper

Avocado Pepita Sauce (page 288)

Anywhere Slaw (page 93)

FOR THE SHRIMP

1 pound / 450 g shrimp, peeled and deveined

1 small red onion, sliced thin

2 jalapeños, sliced, seeded to taste

2 cups / 340 g small cubed pineapple

2 tablespoons avocado or olive oil + more for the pan

1½ tablespoons taco seasoning

1 lime, to finish

Corn tortillas

Cotija cheese

Chopped cilantro

Serves 4

Preheat the oven to 425°F / 220°C.

Combine all the taco seasoning ingredients in a small jar and give it a good shake.

Prepare your Avocado Pepita Sauce and Anywhere Slaw and set aside in the fridge.

Pat the shrimp dry. On an oiled, rimmed baking sheet, combine the shrimp, red onion, jalapeños, pineapple, oil, and taco seasoning. Toss to coat. (This can also be done in a large mixing bowl.) Spread everything in an even layer on the pan. Roast the shrimp on the upper rack for 6 minutes. Turn the heat up to a broil and broil it all for 3 minutes until both the shrimp and pineapple begin to brown on the edges. Remove from the oven and squeeze the lime over the shrimp and toss to coat.

Warm the tortillas, then stuff them with a layer of sauce, some shrimp-pineapple mixture, slaw, and a sprinkle of cotija and cilantro.

Chicken Milanese with Asparagus + Gribiche Salad

Let's dress up a schnitzel! We're basically making a large, adult chicken finger, with a fresh, springy, saucy salad on top. It's everything you need in one dish. While not a classic gribiche, it's a close approximation, with some added asparagus for spring color and freshness.

You can apply this same preparation to 1-inch- / 2.5 cm thick slabs of extra-firm tofu in place of the chicken although tofu is a bit more fragile to work with. An air fryer can get you a crisper crust than the oven should you prefer to bake over pan-frying either option.

FOR THE SALAD

2 tablespoons minced shallot, about 1 small

1 tablespoon champagne vinegar

2 teaspoons extra-virgin olive oil

1 pound / 450 g asparagus, medium stalks

2 teaspoons Dijon mustard

1 tablespoon capers, chopped

2 tablespoons mayonnaise or Vegenaise

2 hard-boiled eggs, minced

¼ cup / 5 g flat-leaf parsley, chopped

1 tablespoon fresh tarragon, chopped

Zest and juice of ½ a lemon

2 cornichons, chopped, optional

½ teaspoon sea salt

½ teaspoon freshly ground pepper

To make the salad, in a mixing bowl, combine the shallot and champagne vinegar. Toss to combine. Set aside to lightly pickle while you prepare the asparagus.

Trim the ends off the asparagus and slice into thin slices, on a generous diagonal. In a large skillet over medium heat, heat a drizzle of the olive oil. Add the asparagus to the hot pan and give it all a shake. Sear the asparagus for 2 to 3 minutes until just tender. Season with a bit of salt and pepper, set aside, and allow to cool slightly. You will use the same pan to cook the chicken.

To the bowl with the shallot mixture, add the mustard, capers, mayonnaise, minced eggs, chopped parsley, and tarragon. Mix and smash everything to combine. Add the asparagus, lemon zest, lemon juice, cornichons (if using), salt, and pepper to the bowl and mix again. Set aside in the fridge until you're ready to serve.

Place the chicken on your cutting board and pound the thick end down to an even (roughly) 1½-inch / 3.75 cm thickness. With a sharp knife, butterfly each breast so you get four thin cutlets. Between two sheets of parchment or wax paper, pound the breasts to an even ½-inch / 12 mm thickness. Season with ½ teaspoon each of salt and pepper.

CONTINUED

Chicken Milanese with Asparagus + Gribiche Salad, continued

continued

FOR THE CHICKEN

2 boneless, skinless chicken breasts (about 1 pound / 450 g)

1 teaspoon sea salt, divided

½ teaspoon freshly ground pepper

⅓ cup / 120 g all-purpose flour

2 large eggs

1 teaspoon Dijon mustard

3 tablespoons / 45 ml milk

1 cup / 135 g panko

1 teaspoon dried oregano

1 teaspoon paprika

3 tablespoons / 45 ml extra-virgin olive oil, divided

1 tablespoon salted butter, divided

Baby arugula

Toasted pine nuts

Freshly ground pepper

Serves 4

Create an assembly with three dishes. In one shallow dish, add the flour. In the second, whisk together the eggs, mustard, and milk until combined. In the third, combine the panko, oregano, remaining ½ teaspoon salt, and paprika. With each piece of chicken, dredge it in the flour, shaking off any excess. Then into the egg mixture, letting excess drip off. Finally, dredge it in the panko, pressing it into the chicken, and set aside.

To cook the chicken, heat 1½ tablespoons of olive oil and ½ tablespoon of butter in the skillet over medium-high heat. Once hot, cook the chicken, two pieces at a time, until golden, about 4 minutes. Flip, and cook on the other side until golden and cooked through. About 8 minutes total (the chicken is thin!). Set aside on a cooling rack to rest while you cook the second batch. Repeat this whole process with the other pieces, adding the remaining oil and butter between batches.

Toss some baby arugula in with the asparagus salad and serve over the top of your chicken. Garnish with toasted pine nuts and a grind of fresh pepper.

CHANGE IT UP
Gluten free: Use a gluten-free flour and panko.

Chicken Parmesan Meatballs

Some of you may notice that these are quite similar to the turkey meatballs from my previous book *Bowl + Spoon*. This version has a bit more structure, so they hold their shape when mixed with noodles or stuffed into a bun to make a meatball sub for the kids. When my kids have been in picky phases, these have always been an easy sell, something everyone will eat. They can be made in advance with nothing lost when reheated, so they also work great for new moms or sick friends.

3 cloves garlic, grated

1 teaspoon fennel seed, roughly chopped

1 teaspoon Italian seasoning

½ teaspoon sea salt

½ teaspoon freshly ground pepper

1 large egg

⅓ cup / 55 g panko

⅓ cup / 35 g grated Parmesan

⅓ cup / 7 g well-chopped flat-leaf parsley + more for garnish

1 tablespoon extra-virgin olive oil + more for cooking

1 pound / 450 g ground chicken, dark meat included

FOR THE POLENTA

1 cup / 200 g polenta

Salt and pepper

2 cups / 475 ml water

2 cups / 475 ml milk

2 tablespoons salted butter

1 (24-ounce / 680 g) jar of marinara

6 ounces / 170 g mozzarella, shredded or torn

½ cup / 50 g grated Parmesan + more for finishing

In a large mixing bowl, combine the garlic, fennel seed, Italian seasoning, salt, pepper, egg, panko, Parmesan, parsley, and oil. Stir to mix well. Add the ground chicken and fold everything in to combine. Let this mixture rest for 15 minutes or in the fridge for up to a day.

Start the polenta. In a large pot over medium heat, combine the polenta, salt, pepper, and water, stir and simmer for 15 minutes. Turn the heat to low, add the milk and continue to simmer, stirring occasionally, for 15 more minutes. We want it to be loose; it firms up as it cools, so add more water or milk for desired consistency. Stir in the butter and taste for seasoning. Cover and set aside.

Preheat the oven to 475°F / 245°C. Warm a thin layer of oil in an ovenproof skillet over medium heat. Form the chicken mixture into small balls and, once the oil is hot, sear the balls. About 3 minutes per side until the outsides are just golden (these can also be roasted for 15 minutes). Turn the heat to low, pour the marinara over the balls, and stir gently. Let the marinara warm up for a few minutes. Put a piece of the mozzarella on top of each ball, plus a sprinkle of Parmesan, and put the pan in the oven for 6 to 8 minutes until the cheese is just golden.

CONTINUED

Chicken Parmesan Meatballs, continued

FOR THE CHARD

2 tablespoons extra-virgin olive oil

3 cloves of garlic, sliced thin

1 large bundle rainbow chard, chopped

Salt and pepper

Squeeze of lemon

Chopped parsley, for serving

Serves 4-6

For the chard, heat the oil in a skillet over medium heat. Add the garlic and let it cook for 30 seconds until fragrant. Add the chard and sauté for 2 to 3 minutes. Sprinkle with salt and pepper, a squeeze of lemon, and set aside off the heat.

Assemble your bowls. Make a pillow of polenta, add a few meatballs with sauce, and put some chard on the side. Finish it all with some fresh herbs and a sprinkle of Parm.

MAKE AHEAD

Do the searing or roasting step, cover them in the marinara, and keep covered in the fridge a day in advance. To finish, bring the dish to room temperature, add the cheese, and add 5 more minutes to the baking step. To freeze, cook them all the way through during that searing step, cool, cover them in sauce, then package and freeze them.

CHANGE IT UP

Dairy free: You can get away without using the cheese; just increase the panko to ½ cup / 65 g and skip the cheese topping. Use a nondairy milk and butter in the polenta.

Gluten free: Almond meal or gluten-free breadcrumbs may be used as a substitute for the panko. I would suggest keeping the balls small.

There's Always Chicken

Whenever I don't know what to make, there is always chicken. I pick a flavor direction, make rice or quinoa or potatoes and whatever vegetable makes sense, and prepare a green salad to round it out.

The recipes below are simple ratios based on cooking **2 pounds / 900 g of boneless, skinless chicken** (which generally feeds four adults with a little left over for lunches). We have people who favor both chicken breasts and thighs here, so I usually do a mix, given that I am likely chopping them all up anyway. Pound thicker breasts down to 1-inch / 2.5 cm thickness for even cooking.

I can usually leave the thighs alone, but pound those if they are thick as well. Stir the marinade ingredients together in a mixing bowl or large ziplock bag and add the chicken, and mix to coat. Marinate overnight if you can, but at least a couple hours in the fridge. Grill, pan-fry, or roast the chicken on high heat until just cooked through (buy a meat thermometer!). Let it rest and chop it up in its own juices. Drizzle with the pan drippings, or a little olive oil and a fresh squeeze of citrus, after the chop to keep it hydrated.

House Favorite

3 tablespoons / 45 g mild harissa paste

1 tablespoon tamari or soy sauce

2 tablespoons rice vinegar

4 cloves garlic, grated

1 teaspoon paprika

¼ cup / 60 ml avocado oil

2 tablespoons agave nectar

1 teaspoon sea salt

Freshly ground pepper

Asian Vibes

1 tablespoon gochujang

2 tablespoons coconut aminos

Dash of fish sauce

1 tablespoon brown sugar

⅓ cup / 80 ml soy sauce or tamari

2 tablespoons toasted sesame oil

2 tablespoons rice vinegar

½ teaspoon sea salt

Freshly ground pepper

Italian Vibes

¼ cup / 60 ml balsamic vinegar

2 tablespoons brown sugar

2 teaspoons Dijon mustard

4 cloves garlic, grated

¼ cup / 60 ml extra-virgin olive oil

Zest of 1 lemon

2 teaspoons dried Italian seasoning

Pinch of red pepper flakes

1 teaspoon sea salt

Freshly ground pepper

Mexi Vibes

¼ cup / 60 ml avocado oil

2 tablespoons agave nectar

Zest of 2 limes

4 cloves garlic, grated

½ cup / 10 g chopped cilantro

2 teaspoons chili powder

2 teaspoons cumin

2 tablespoons hot sauce

1 teaspoon sea salt

Freshly ground pepper

Hippy Vibes

⅓ cup / 75 g plain yogurt

¼ cup / 60 ml olive oil

1 teaspoon turmeric powder

3-inch / 7.5 cm piece of fresh ginger, grated

2 tablespoons coconut aminos

1 teaspoon garlic powder

1 teaspoon red pepper flakes

1 tablespoon honey

1 teaspoon sea salt

Freshly ground pepper

Italian Turkey Burgers with Frico Crisps

Even as the cook of a burger-loving household, I find the charm of the classic preparation has its limits. There's room to shake things up. These go well with Mixed Roasted Potatoes (page 131) or Lemon and Parm Broccoli (page 121).

You can swap four Roma tomatoes in place of the bell peppers if that is more your jam. Both bring that juicy layer that a turkey burger needs.

My kids say they hate olives, but they don't notice them once everything is mixed in (it's really not that much), so give it a rumble if yours say the same.

FOR THE BURGERS

2 tablespoons minced shallot

2 teaspoons extra-virgin olive oil

2 cloves garlic, minced

½ teaspoon sea salt, divided

½ teaspoon Italian seasoning

½ teaspoon ground fennel seed

Pinch of red pepper flakes

⅓ cup / 80 g prepared olive tapenade

Zest of 1 small lemon

⅓ cup / 7 g chopped basil

1 pound / 450 g ground turkey or chicken, not extra lean

FOR THE ROASTED PEPPERS

2 red bell peppers

2 tablespoons extra-virgin olive oil

2 cloves garlic, grated

½ teaspoon Italian seasoning

Pinch of red pepper flakes

Sea salt

Freshly ground pepper

Preheat the oven to 375°F / 190°C.

In a sauté pan over medium heat, sauté the shallot in the olive oil for 4 minutes, add the garlic, half the salt, Italian seasoning, fennel seed, and pepper flakes and cook for another minute. Transfer everything to a large bowl and allow to cool a bit, scraping the pan of all those toasty seasonings. Stir in the olive tapenade, lemon zest, and basil. Add the turkey and mix until just combined. Chill in the fridge for at least 15 minutes, preferably an hour, or overnight if you're prepping ahead.

Trim the peppers and cut each one into quarters. On a parchment paper–lined baking sheet, arrange the peppers cut-side up, season with the oil, garlic, Italian seasoning, red pepper flakes, salt, and pepper, and rub it all over to coat. Roast for 30 minutes until caramelized and collapsed. Remove from the oven to cool.

Turn the oven up to 400°F / 200°C. Prep a large baking sheet with parchment or a Silpat.

CONTINUED

Italian Turkey Burgers with Frico Crisps, continued

FOR THE FRICO CRISPS

½ cup / 50 g freshly grated Parmesan

1 tablespoon lemon zest

½ teaspoon Italian seasoning

4 or 5 ciabatta rolls, focaccia, or soft brioche buns

Mayonnaise

3 cups / 60 g baby arugula

Everyday Pesto (page 280), optional

Serves 4–5

In a small bowl, combine the Parm, lemon zest, and Italian seasoning. Transfer a heaping 2-tablespoon pile of the mix on the sheet. Repeat, keeping the piles 2 inches / 5 cm apart to allow for spreading. Bake for 5 minutes until golden. If you're short on time, you can skip this step, but they're lovely.

Preheat a cast-iron skillet over medium-high heat. Form the turkey mix into four or five patties, and sprinkle with a bit more salt and pepper. Sear for 5 minutes, flip, and cook for an additional 4 to 5 minutes, until cooked through. Toast the buns.

To serve, spread a spoonful of mayo on the bottom bun, add the burger, and top with roasted peppers, frico, and arugula. Spread a generous amount of pesto or more tapenade on the top bun and smash everything together.

MAKE AHEAD
The roasted peppers and the burger mix can be prepared a day in advance.

CHANGE IT UP
Vegetarian: These work with ground Beyond Beef, and will just need a few more minutes of cooking time.

Harissa Lamb Meatballs with Couscous

Make these tasty meatballs into a meal for company by serving them with Smoky Eggplant Dip (page 58), some good naan, and a green salad. Admittedly, the spices and condiments are crossing over a few different types of cuisines, but I think it works!

Harissa paste has a bit of heat but is still passable for my kids, especially if I smash the meatballs into the couscous. Every brand will vary; Mina is a well-known brand that makes a mild version. Trader Joe's sells one that is a bit spicier.

FOR THE MEATBALLS

1 tablespoon mild harissa paste

1 large egg, beaten

½ cup / 135 g panko

3 cloves garlic, grated

½ cup / 10 g finely chopped parsley

1 tablespoon extra-virgin olive oil

½ teaspoon sea salt

½ teaspoon freshly ground pepper

1 pound / 450 g ground lamb

FOR THE SAUCE

2 tablespoons unsalted butter or olive oil

½ a small yellow onion, diced

2 cloves garlic, grated

¼ teaspoon cinnamon

½ teaspoon coriander

1 teaspoon paprika

1 tablespoon tomato paste

1 teaspoon mild harissa paste

1 (28-ounce / 800 g) can crushed tomatoes

1 teaspoon sea salt

½ teaspoon freshly ground pepper

In a large mixing bowl, combine the harissa, egg, panko, and garlic and stir to mix. Add the parsley, oil, salt, pepper, and lamb and use your hands or a fork to mix until just combined. Cover and set aside in the fridge.

Preheat the oven to 425°F / 220°C. Line a rimmed baking sheet with parchment paper.

In a large shallow skillet over medium-low heat, melt the butter. Once melted, add the onion and sauté for 2 to 3 minutes, or until translucent. Add the garlic, cinnamon, coriander, and paprika. Stir to combine and toast for another minute, just until fragrant. Add the tomato paste and stir to combine. While stirring, slowly add the crushed tomatoes, harissa, and salt and pepper. Bring the mixture to a gentle simmer and cover while you prepare the rest.

Roll the lamb meatballs into about 2-tablespoon-size balls and line them up on the prepared baking sheet. Transfer to the oven, and roast on the middle rack for 15 minutes. Once cooked, carefully transfer the meatballs into the tomato-sauce mixture, cover, and gently simmer for 10 minutes until all warmed through.

CONTINUED

Harissa Lamb Meatballs with Couscous, continued

1 tablespoon extra-virgin olive oil

½ a small yellow onion, diced

1¼ cups / 300 ml vegetable broth

1 cup / 170 g couscous

½ teaspoon sea salt

½ teaspoon freshly ground pepper

Butter

8 dried apricots, finely chopped

¼ cup / 5 g finely chopped fresh parsley

½ cup / 10 g fresh mint, chopped, for serving

Feta cheese, for garnish, optional

Serves 4

While the meatballs finish cooking, make your couscous. In a pot over medium heat, warm the oil. Add the onion and a big pinch of salt and sauté until translucent, about 3 minutes. Add the broth and bring it to a gentle simmer. Stir in the couscous, turn off the heat, cover, and let it sit for 10 minutes to absorb the liquid. Fluff the couscous with a fork, season with salt and pepper, add a nub of butter, and stir in the dried apricots and parsley.

Serve the meatballs with couscous and a sprinkle of mint and feta over the top.

MAKE AHEAD
The day before, mix up the meatball ingredients and store in the fridge.

CHANGE IT UP
Gluten free: Sub in quinoa for the couscous (adjusting the cooking time to package instructions).

Dairy free: You can use olive oil instead of butter here and a dairy free feta cheese.

French Bread Pizzas

I can think of a good two-to-three-year stretch of my childhood where we ate frozen Stouffer's French Bread Pizzas a few times a week. I would bet they sold them at Costco, because my mom always stocked the freezer with their quick frozen items.

Think of this as your upgrade: the convenience of layering things on a split French baguette, but with an amazing sauce, a layer of vegetables and prosciutto, and a finish of hot honey.

Serve this with a crunchy green salad—maybe more fennel, orange segments, some arugula, and our Double Mustard Maple Dressing (page 289). You could qualify this as an appetizer if you cut the pizza into smaller pieces.

1 baguette

1 tablespoon extra-virgin olive oil

1 large fennel bulb, halved, cored and shaved thin, fronds reserved

1 bell pepper, cut in matchsticks

2 shallots, sliced thin

Salt and freshly ground pepper

Romesco-ish sauce (page 286)

4 ounces / 113 g serrano ham or prosciutto, sliced into ribbons

8 ounces / 227 g grated Manchego cheese

½ cup / 50 g grated Parmesan

1 teaspoon red pepper flakes

2 tablespoons hot honey

Fresh parsley, for garnish

Grated Parmesan cheese, for garnish

Serves 4

Preheat the oven to 425°F / 220°C. Slice the baguette in half lengthwise and lay it on a rimmed baking sheet. Toast in the oven for just a minute.

Heat a skillet over medium heat with a drizzle of olive oil. Add the fennel, pepper, and shallots along with a pinch of salt and pepper. Sauté until just tender, about 3 minutes.

Spread a layer of sauce on each baguette half. Distribute the sautéed vegetables between them as well as the prosciutto ribbons. Sprinkle the cheeses over both sides and top with a sprinkle of red pepper flakes.

Bake on the middle rack for 10 minutes, until everything is warmed through and the cheese bubbles a bit. Out of the oven, drizzle hot honey over the top. Garnish with fresh parsley, a sprinkle of Parm, and fennel fronds. Cut into pieces.

MAKE AHEAD
The Romesco-ish sauce can be made up to 5 days in advance.

Spring Spaghetti with Asparagus + Peas

I like noodles as a vehicle for vegetables, so excuse me while I take the intentions of a carbonara and add too many spring vegetables. I'll serve smaller portions of this with a big green salad or perhaps a whole roasted chicken if I'm filling out a meal for company.

1 large egg

2 egg yolks

½ cup / 50 g finely grated pecorino cheese + more for garnish

Salt and pepper

12 ounces / 340 g spaghetti

1 pound / 450 g asparagus, trimmed, cut in 2-inch / 5 cm pieces (if your asparagus is on the thicker side, slice them in half lengthwise as well)

½ cup / 65 g fresh or frozen peas

2 tablespoons extra-virgin olive oil

2 tablespoons unsalted butter

1 tablespoon capers, drained and roughly chopped

3 large cloves garlic, grated

½ teaspoon freshly ground pepper

Zest and juice of 1 small lemon

½ cup / 62 g toasted pistachios, chopped

Fresh chopped parsley and mint

Serves 4

Bring a large pot of generously salted water to a boil.

In a mixing bowl, whisk the egg, egg yolks, the cheese, and a pinch of salt and black pepper and set aside.

Cook the pasta according to package instructions. Drain, reserving 2 cups / 480 ml of the pasta water. Whisk ½ cup / 120 ml of the pasta water into the egg mixture to temper it.

Put the pot back over medium heat and warm the olive oil and butter. Add the capers and grated garlic, and sauté until just fragrant, about 1 minute. Add the asparagus and peas and sauté for a few minutes, until tender. Turn the heat to low and transfer the noodles to the pot. Add the pepper, ½ cup / 120 ml of the pasta water, and a few generous pinches of salt, and toss everything to combine. Take the pot off the heat, slowly tip the contents of the egg bowl into the pot, and toss again until the noodles are coated in a glossy sauce. Add more pasta water as needed, a small splash at a time. This takes about 2 minutes; just keep gently tossing and it will get there. There should be a bit of puddling in the bottom and that is fine. We want it saucy—the noodles drink it up as they rest. Add the lemon zest and juice of half the lemon and toss again. Taste for salt and pepper.

Serve immediately. Garnish with more cheese, the pistachios, parsley, and mint.

THE Veggie Burger with Roasted Tomatoes + Quick Pickles

These veggie burgers are perfect with all the sauces and pickles and toasty tomato. My kids will eat these without complaint—hold the pickles and tomato of course. That said, don't skip the recipe if you don't have all the toppings; they are great pared down too. I love a leftover patty as a snack with whatever sauce is around or some smashed avocado, and they store well if you want extras for later.

These burgers are too delicate to grill, so I bake them, but if you have a griddle, I could see cooking these on there.

FOR THE QUICK PICKLES

½ cup / 120 ml white vinegar

¼ cup / 60 ml water

1 tablespoon cane sugar

Pinch of mustard seeds

2 cloves garlic, smashed

1 teaspoon sea salt

2 tablespoons fresh dill, chopped

3 Kirby or Persian cucumbers, thinly sliced lengthwise

½ a red onion, thinly sliced

FOR THE ROASTED TOMATOES

4 Roma tomatoes, halved lengthwise, seeded

1 tablespoon olive oil

Pinch of salt and pepper

Pinch of dried Italian seasoning

FOR THE BURGER MIX

2 cloves garlic, roughly chopped

1 small shallot, roughly chopped

⅓ cup / 40 g walnut pieces

1 large egg

1 tablespoon tomato paste

1 tablespoon Dijon mustard

2 tablespoons olive oil + more for cooking

In a small pot over medium heat, warm the vinegar, water, sugar, mustard seeds, garlic, and salt. Stir until the sugar is dissolved, about 1 minute, and take it off the heat. Put the dill, cucumbers, and onion in a small bowl or glass jar, pour the warm vinegar mixture over the top, and stir to combine. Set the quick pickles aside to cool. Store covered in the fridge if you make these ahead.

Preheat the oven to 325°F / 165°C. Line a rimmed baking sheet with parchment paper. Toss the tomatoes with the oil, salt, pepper, and Italian seasoning. Place them cut-side up on the baking sheet and roast for 30 minutes. Remove from the sheet and set aside, reserving the baking sheet.

Meanwhile, make the patties. Heat a small skillet over medium heat with a drizzle of olive oil. Give the garlic, shallot, and walnuts a quick sauté to just toast, about 3 minutes. In a food processor, combine the sautéed garlic, shallot, walnuts, and egg. Pulse to chop. Add the tomato paste, Dijon, olive oil, panko, parsley, paprika, salt, and a few grinds of fresh pepper and pulse again. Scoop out 1 cup / 240 ml of sweet potato flesh from the baked potato and add it along with the rice and beans. Give it all just five to ten more pulses to combine. We want the pieces of rice and beans to be distinguishable, but for it to have some hold (like the texture of meatballs).

CONTINUED

THE Veggie Burger with Roasted Tomatoes
+ Quick Pickles, continued

⅓ cup / 60 g panko or pulsed oats

1 cup / 20 g flat-leaf parsley, chopped

2 teaspoons paprika

1 teaspoon sea salt

Freshly ground pepper

1 large sweet potato, baked and cooled

1 cup / 200 g cooked and cooled brown rice

1 (14-ounce / 400 g) can black beans, rinsed and drained

Sliced cheese, optional

Brioche buns

Mayonnaise

Mustard

2 avocados, sliced

Baby arugula

Serves 6

Turn the oven up to 425°F / 220°C. Wipe down your tomato baking sheet and line it with parchment paper. Form the burgers into six (1-inch / 2.5 cm thick) patties. Brush or spray the tops with oil and bake them for 15 to 18 minutes until you get a golden crust on the bottom. Turn off the heat, put the cheese over the top (if using), and put them back in the still-warm oven just to melt the cheese.

Toast your buns. Spread each side with mayo and mustard, smash avocado onto your bottom bun, then layer with a patty, some arugula, roasted tomatoes, quick pickles, and close her up! Repeat and enjoy.

CHANGE IT UP
There was a food truck our family visited that served a "dirty veggie burger," which was a veggie burger with bacon. As someone who does eat meat but prefers a veg burger patty, this is a pretty great combo.

The Avocado Pepita Sauce (page 288) or Another Green Sauce (page 286) with a little mayo stirred in are excellent here as well, if you have the time. Omit the sliced avocado if you're using the Avocado Pepita Sauce.

Vegan: You can replace the egg with a flax egg (1 tablespoon flaxmeal mixed with 3 tablespoons water).

MAKE AHEAD
The burger mixture and quick pickles can be made up to a day ahead. Keep covered in the fridge.

Pasta with Roasted Cauliflower, Chorizo + Winter Pesto

A dish that has excellent ROI with your cooking time, it is also filling and textured *and* has lots of vegetables. You may have a little bit more kale pesto than you need for this recipe, but it has other uses, such as with eggs, atop roasted potatoes, or as a veggie sandwich spread. We don't want the fresh sausage-like chorizo in tube form; instead, look for a dry chorizo, typically from Spain, not Mexico, that you will find in a well-stocked cheese section. It looks like salami.

FOR THE KALE PESTO

2 cloves garlic

¼ cup / 30 g pine nuts

2 tablespoons lemon juice

1 cup / 30 g cilantro or parsley

1 packed cup / 25 g de-ribbed and chopped lacinato kale

1 teaspoon sea salt

½ teaspoon freshly ground pepper

⅓ cup / 60 ml extra-virgin olive oil

¼ cup / 25 g grated Parmesan cheese

FOR THE CAULIFLOWER

1 head cauliflower, broken into small florets

3 tablespoons / 35 ml extra-virgin olive oil

½ teaspoon dried oregano

Sea salt and freshly ground pepper

2 ounces / 55 g dried chorizo, cut in 1-inch / 2.5 cm pieces

1 small bundle lacinato kale, de-ribbed and cut into ribbons

12 ounces / 340 g any short pasta

Half of 1 lemon

Grated Parmesan

Red pepper flakes

Fresh chopped parsley

Serves 4

Make the kale pesto. In a food processor, pulse the garlic, pine nuts, and lemon juice together. Add the cilantro or parsley, kale, salt, and pepper and run again until extra chopped. With the motor going, add the olive oil and Parmesan cheese. Set aside.

Bring a large pot of salted water to a boil.

Preheat the oven to 425°F / 220°C. On a rimmed baking sheet, pile the cauliflower florets and drizzle them with the oil, oregano, salt, and pepper. Toss well to coat and roast for 30 minutes until the edges are toasty. To the baking sheet, add the chorizo slivers and kale and toss it all around to coat in some of the residual oils, adding a little more if the sheet looks dry. Roast an additional 3 minutes to warm.

Cook the pasta according to instructions. Reserve about ½ cup / 120 ml of the pasta water. Drain the pasta, then put it back in the pot with a few heaping spoonfuls of the pesto and a big splash of pasta water. Stir to mix; we want it generously sauced. Add the contents of the baking sheet and a squeeze of lemon and stir again to mix. Stir in more pesto if you'd like, or pasta water as needed to loosen things up.

Serve portions with a generous sprinkling of Parmesan cheese, red pepper flakes, a grind of fresh pepper, and fresh chopped parsley.

MAKE AHEAD
The kale pesto can be made a few days in advance.

CHANGE IT UP
Vegetarian: Replace the chorizo with some chopped sundried tomatoes.

Taco Salad with Roasted Jalapeño Ranch

This salad can be a side for taco night or a meal in itself with the addition of some grilled chicken or salmon, or cooked quinoa to keep it vegetarian. I'll wrap these goodies in warm tortillas for the kids and leave it as salad bowls for me and Hugh, and everyone eats without complaint.

Depending on the season, butternut squash can be used in place of the sweet potatoes and requires the same prep and cooking time. I know I just casually slid in "grilled corn" as an ingredient like it doesn't require an extra step, but I love those char marks popping up in the salad. It's the little things. This can be done by rotating the corn around in a hot oven too!

FOR THE SWEET POTATOES

2 medium sweet potatoes, diced

2 tablespoons extra-virgin olive oil

1 tablespoon maple syrup

1 teaspoon chili powder

½ teaspoon sea salt

FOR THE DRESSING

1 jalapeño

2 cloves of garlic, chopped

2 teaspoons honey

1 teaspoon Dijon mustard

Dash of Worcestershire

1 bunch of cilantro

1 teaspoon onion powder

½ teaspoon dried dill

½ teaspoon cumin

1 teaspoon sea salt

Pinch of paprika

2 limes, zest and juice

2 teaspoons white wine vinegar

⅓ cup / 90 ml mayonnaise

½ cup / 120 g sour cream or whole milk Greek yogurt

¼ teaspoon freshly ground black pepper

Preheat the oven to 400°F / 200°C. Put your potatoes on a rimmed baking sheet. Drizzle them with the oil, maple syrup, chili powder, and salt. Toss everything well to coat and spread in a single layer. Roast for 25 minutes, stirring halfway through, until just tender, then remove to cool.

While the potatoes roast, make the dressing. Roast the jalapeño by charring it over the stove flame or roasting it under the broiler until blackened on all sides. Wrap in plastic wrap to cool, then peel away the charred skin. It doesn't need to be perfect. Chop. In a blender or food processor, combine the pepper (partially seeded if you don't want a spice kick) and the rest of the dressing ingredients. Pulse everything until mostly smooth and you can see small green flecks. Transfer to a jar and keep in the fridge until ready to use.

CONTINUED

1 head romaine, torn or sliced

2 cups / 140 g shredded cabbage

2 radishes, shaved paper thin

1 bunch cilantro, chopped

1 cup / 170 g cooked and rinsed black beans

1 cup / 150 g grilled corn

⅓ cup / 90 g roasted, salted pepitas, divided

¼ cup / 30 g diced red onion, rinsed and drained

1 red bell pepper, finely diced

2 ripe but firm avocados, diced

3 ounces / 85 g cotija cheese, crumbled

Tortilla chips

Serves 4

Assemble your salad. In a large mixing bowl, combine the romaine, cabbage, radishes, cilantro, beans, corn, half of the pepitas, onion, and bell pepper. Drizzle desired amount of dressing and toss everything to coat.

Transfer to bowls and top with the roasted potatoes, remaining pepitas, and avocado. Finish with a sprinkle of cheese and tortilla chips.

MAKE AHEAD
The roasted jalapeño ranch will keep in the fridge for 1 to 2 weeks.

Tofu + Mushroom Lettuce Wraps

I like to use lemongrass in the mixture here, which (to save you the market scavenger hunt) can generally be found by the small aromatics like shallots or fresh herbs. To prepare the lemongrass, you want to remove the outer layer, smash it with the side of a knife, and mince. It adds a unique brightness that is hard to replicate with anything else.

This same tofu mixture is also great in a rice bowl and can easily be doubled, making it an easy family-style dinner for a group. Not vegetarian? Add some ground pork in with the tofu, along with more oil and tamari, to stretch this further.

3 tablespoons / 45 ml coconut or avocado oil, divided

8 ounces / 225 g mushrooms, wiped cleaned and minced

Salt

15 ounces / 425 g extra-firm tofu, drained

½ a small red onion, finely chopped

1 tablespoon toasted sesame oil

3 cloves garlic, minced

1 serrano or jalapeño pepper, partially seeded and minced

1 stalk lemongrass, minced

2 tablespoons tamari or soy sauce

2 teaspoons fish sauce

1 tablespoon honey

Zest and juice of 1 lime

3 green onions, thinly sliced

2 tablespoons chili crisp

⅓ cup / 74 g Vegenaise or mayonnaise

Dash of rice vinegar

Butter lettuce leaves

Toasted cashews, chopped

Shaved radishes

Fresh mint

Serves 4

Heat half of the oil in a large skillet over medium heat. Add the mushrooms and a big pinch of salt and sauté until most of their liquid is absorbed and edges are browned, about 5 minutes. Remove from the pan and set aside.

Put the remaining oil in the pan, break up the tofu, and add it to the hot pan, breaking it up further with a wooden spoon (like you would ground meat). Let it sit for 5 minutes to get some good browning. Add the onion, sesame oil, garlic, serrano, and lemongrass and sauté another 5 or so minutes to mix. Add the mushrooms back in and stir. Add the tamari, fish sauce, and honey and mix to combine. Turn the heat down and let the flavors absorb for another 5 minutes. Stir in the lime zest, lime juice, and the green onions. Turn off the heat and set aside.

In a small bowl, mix the chili crisp, Vegenaise or mayo, and rice vinegar together and stir to mix.

Arrange a family-style assembly with lettuce leaves, tofu mixture, chili crisp sauce, toasted cashews, radishes, and mint.

Cauliflower Al Pastor Bowls

Heavily spiced cauliflower paired with some sweet roasted pineapple and a creamy sauce—all the flavors are here! My beloved SK Cooking Club folks rave that this is their favorite dish to make when there is a vegetarian or vegan eater as a dinner guest, while keeping the omnivores happy. I serve this as a bowl, but it could just as easily go in a warm tortilla or be scooped up with chips.

FOR THE CAULIFLOWER

¼ cup / 60 ml avocado or olive oil

3 tablespoons / 45 ml pineapple juice

2 teaspoons sauce from a can of chipotle peppers in adobo

1½ teaspoons sea salt

2 teaspoons smoked paprika

2 teaspoons cumin

1 teaspoon chili powder

1 teaspoon dried oregano

1 teaspoon garlic powder

1 large head cauliflower, about 1¼ pounds / 570 g (about 6 cups small florets)

2 cups / 340 g fresh pineapple

1 tablespoon honey

FOR THE AVOCADO CREMA

2 large avocados

1 tablespoon sour cream

¼ cup / 60 ml lime juice

½ of a jalapeño, seeded and minced

¾ teaspoon sea salt, to taste

½ cup / 10 g chopped cilantro

¼ cup / 20 g minced red onion

½ of a jalapeño, seeded and minced

Steamed rice

Greens or Anywhere Slaw (page 93)

Toasted, salted pepitas

Cotija cheese, optional

Limes, cut into wedges

Serves 4

Preheat the oven to 400°F / 200°C.

In a large bowl, whisk together the oil, pineapple juice, adobo sauce, salt, and all the spices until the mixture is smooth. Break the cauliflower into small florets and toss to coat in the spiced oil mixture. Transfer the cauliflower to a large, rimmed baking sheet. Roast for 25 minutes, stirring halfway through. Remove the sheet and turn the heat up to 425°F / 220°C. Give the cauliflower a stir and push it over to make room for the pineapple and squeeze it onto one-third of the pan. Drizzle the honey over the top of the fruit. Pop the pan back in the oven for another 15 minutes until the cauliflower is tender and golden on the edges.

While things bake, make the avocado crema. Mash up the avocados and stir in the sour cream, lime juice, jalapeño, and sea salt until smooth. Set aside.

Dice the roasted pineapple and stir it together with the cilantro, onion, jalapeño, and a few pinches of salt and pepper.

To assemble, make a big swoosh of the avocado crema. Add a scoop of rice, greens, cauliflower, pineapple, toasted pepitas, cotija (if using), and more cilantro. Serve with lime wedges on the side.

CHANGE IT UP
Skip the sour cream and cotija to make these bowls dairy free and vegan.

MAKE AHEAD
Some advance chopping of the cauliflower and pineapple, as well as mixing up your spice blend, will help this meal come together quickly.

Roasted Eggplant Rollups

These rollups are a great side dish or vegetarian main. Should you have picky kids, tuck extra filling into some prepared pizza dough to make them little calzones. If you're not an eggplant fan, you can do the same thing with thin slices of zucchini; they'll just be smaller and require slightly less cooking time.

FOR THE EGGPLANT

2 medium eggplants

1 teaspoon sea salt

3 tablespoons / 45 ml extra-virgin olive oil

1 teaspoon dried Italian seasoning

FOR THE FILLING

4 ounces / 113 g goat cheese, room temperature

8 ounces / 225 g whole milk ricotta

1 large egg

¼ cup / 25 g grated Parmesan + more for finishing

3 cloves garlic, grated

½ cup / 10 g chopped parsley and basil + more for garnish

1 tablespoon lemon zest

Pinch of red pepper flakes

½ teaspoon sea salt

1 teaspoon dried Italian seasoning

½ teaspoon freshly ground pepper

1 (24-ounce / 709 ml) jar marinara sauce, store-bought or homemade

½ cup / 85 g panko

½ cup / 50 g grated Parmesan cheese + more for topping

2 tablespoons extra-virgin olive oil

¼ cup / 30 g toasted pine nuts

Serves 4–6

Cut the ends off the eggplant and slice them into even, ¼-inch / 64 cm slices lengthwise, discarding the end pieces. Season them with salt and put them in a colander to sit for 20 minutes, until they release some water. Preheat the oven to 425°F / 220°C.

Press the water out of the eggplants between a dish towel or paper towels. Lay the slices on two rimmed baking sheets and brush both sides with olive oil. Season with the dried Italian seasoning. Roast the eggplant for 15 to 17 minutes, flipping them over halfway through, until just tender. Remove to cool. Turn the oven down to 375°F / 190°C.

While the eggplant slices cool, make the filling. Mix together the goat cheese, ricotta, egg, Parmesan, garlic, parsley and basil, lemon zest, red pepper flakes, salt, Italian seasoning, and pepper.

Spread 1 cup / 240 ml of the marinara in the bottom of a baking dish. Spread 2 or 3 tablespoons of the cheese mixture across a slice of eggplant, covering the surface. Gently roll it up like a little pinwheel. Place seam side down in the marinara and repeat with your remaining eggplant slices. Spoon the remaining marinara over the top.

In a small bowl, mix the panko, Parmesan, and olive oil together until the crumbs are evenly coated. Sprinkle the topping over the top of the eggplants. Pop the pan back into the oven on the middle rack for 15 to 20 minutes to warm everything through. Turn the broiler on for 1 minute just to crisp the topping. Watch carefully so it does not burn!

Garnish the top with fresh herbs and pine nuts. Allow the dish to rest for 10 minutes before serving.

MAKE AHEAD
Mix the filling a day in advance.

Mushroom "Carnitas"

We frequent a taco shop that makes a vegetarian taco full of sautéed mushrooms. They don't cook off all their water, so the mushrooms are slimy and tasteless. I'm an irritating lunch date because I will eat it but continue to discourse about how it could be made better. *This* is what should go in a mushroom taco! Mushrooms cook down so, so much. It will look like a lot of mushrooms to start, but it moderately feeds two adults and two kids here . . . ones who won't really eat mushrooms. These are so intensely packed with flavor—salty and savory with crisp edges from the oven's heat—that these days we prefer them to real-deal carnitas.

These make an excellent taco filling, nacho topping, or a burrito bowl with the Anywhere Slaw on page 93. They are also included in the quesadillas on page 69.

1 pound / 450 g oyster mushrooms

2 tablespoons avocado oil

¼ teaspoon Worcestershire sauce

2 tablespoons orange juice

1 teaspoon hot sauce

½ teaspoon chili powder

½ teaspoon garlic powder

½ teaspoon dried oregano

½ teaspoon sea salt

Freshly ground pepper

Tortillas

Avocado

Finely shredded cabbage

Black beans

Salsa

Cotija

Everything Cashew Sauce (page 287) or Avocado Pepita Sauce (page 288)

Serves 2

Preheat the oven to 400°F / 200°C. Arrange your taco fixings, because these move pretty quick.

On a baking sheet, shred up all the mushrooms with two forks. In a small bowl, mix the oil, Worcestershire, orange juice, hot sauce, chili powder, garlic powder, oregano, salt, and pepper together. Drizzle it over the mushroom shreds and toss to coat. It will look a bit dry, but it will work! Spread them in an even layer.

Roast the mushrooms for 15 minutes, toss them around, scraping up any brown bits, and roast another 5 to 7 minutes. You should have browning and crisp edges.

Assemble your tacos with warm tortillas, avocado, cabbage, beans, salsa, cotija, and mushrooms. Serve with Everything Cashew Sauce or Avocado Pepita Sauce.

CHANGE IT UP
Skip the cotija to make this dairy free and vegan.

Butternut Steaks with Green Apple Relish

This was made with the fall and winter holidays in mind. I'm just not really a traditional-American-Thanksgiving-sides type of gal, and I also feel that color is underrepresented at those holiday meals. It's obviously an anytime dinner, but if you're short on ideas for vegetarian mains for a fall or winter holiday, this is a really good one.

Cutting a butternut squash is not for the faint of heart. First, please sharpen your knife! We are using the neck of the squash for our "steaks," so choose one that is wide enough to get a few slabs from. Save the bulb portion for another use.

FOR THE QUINOA

1 cup / 140 g quinoa, rinsed and drained

1½ cups / 360 ml vegetable broth

½ teaspoon dried Italian seasoning

1 tablespoon extra-virgin olive oil

1 tablespoon champagne vinegar

3 ounces / 85 g baby arugula

FOR THE APPLE RELISH

1 large green or Honeycrisp apple, finely diced

1 jalapeño, mostly seeded, minced

¼ red onion, minced

⅓ cup / 7 g cilantro, chopped

1 handful mint leaves, chopped

Juice of 1 lime

½ teaspoon sea salt

Freshly ground pepper

Start the quinoa. Put the rinsed quinoa and broth into a pot and bring it to a simmer. Cover and cook for 12 minutes. Once cooked, fluff it with a fork, turn off the heat, put the cover back on ajar, and set it aside to finish steaming off the heat. When it is no longer steaming, stir in the Italian seasoning, oil, and vinegar, then add the arugula and toss to combine.

While the quinoa cooks, make the relish. Put the diced apple in a bowl along with the jalapeño, onion, cilantro, mint, lime, and a few pinches of salt and pepper. Stir to mix and set aside.

Preheat the oven to 375°F / 190°C. Line a rimmed baking sheet with parchment paper (for easy cleanup) with a cooling rack on top, if you have one. Not a huge deal if you don't, just helps the squash stay crisp.

CONTINUED

Butternut Steaks with Green Apple Relish, continued

FOR THE SPICE PASTE

3 tablespoons / 45 ml extra-virgin olive oil

1 teaspoon brown sugar

1 teaspoon smoked paprika

½ teaspoon onion powder

½ teaspoon Aleppo pepper (or chili powder)

1 teaspoon sea salt

Freshly ground pepper

2 medium butternut squashes (roughly 1 pound / 450 g each)

Avocado oil, for cooking

4 ounces / 113 g goat cheese

Serves 4

To make the spice paste, whisk the oil, brown sugar, smoked paprika, onion powder, Aleppo pepper, salt, and some pepper in a large mixing bowl.

Cut the bulb end off the squash and save it for another use. Peel the long cylindrical part of the squash. Stand it upright and carefully cut down, lengthwise, in ½-inch- / 1.25 cm thick slabs of squash. You should get three or four per squash, some with rounded ends that are still edible, just not "steaks" for presentation's sake. Toss them all in the spice paste mixture.

Heat a drizzle of avocado or other high heat oil in a large skillet over medium heat. Add a layer of squash and sear for about 4 minutes per side until you see some brown marks. Transfer the squash to the rack on your baking sheet and bake for another 15 to 20 minutes until tender through to the center.

On a platter, layer the quinoa mixture, the slabs of butternut squash, and the apple relish, and finish by sprinkling the goat cheese over the top.

MAKE AHEAD

The apple relish and quinoa can be made a day in advance.

CHANGE IT UP

Vegan: Just skip the cheese and add some toasted pistachios or almonds for fat and texture in its place.

Winter Bowls with Green Tahini

Yes, there are two condiments up top here, and that will make for a bit of extra prep, but you can make those things in advance so it won't feel like so many pieces at once.

I prefer to use low, shallow bowls for serving here, so all the goodies are close at hand and don't fall into the depths. If you have the time, the tofu benefits from a thirty-minute-to-overnight marinade.

Green Tahini (page 283)

Quick Pickled Onions
(page 289)

FOR THE TOFU

1 (13-ounce / 368 g) block
extra-firm tofu, excess water
pressed out

2 tablespoons avocado oil

1 tablespoon balsamic vinegar

1 tablespoon soy sauce or tamari

1 teaspoon garlic powder

½ teaspoon dried oregano

Pinch of cayenne

½ teaspoon sea salt

½ teaspoon freshly ground pepper

FOR THE VEGETABLES

12 ounces / 340 g baby potatoes,
halved

1 medium head of cauliflower,
broken into small florets

4 tablespoons / 60 ml
extra-virgin olive oil

1 teaspoon sea salt

½ teaspoon freshly ground pepper

1 teaspoon garlic powder

1 teaspoon paprika

1 teaspoon dried oregano

Start by making your condiments and set aside in the fridge until ready to assemble.

Preheat the oven to 425°F / 220°C. Line one of two rimmed baking sheets with parchment paper.

Cube the tofu into ½-inch / 1.25 cm cubes. Put it in a mixing bowl and drizzle with the oil, balsamic, soy sauce, garlic powder, oregano, and cayenne and season with salt and pepper. Gently toss to coat. Marinate for 30 minutes if you can while you prep the potatoes and cauliflower.

Put the baby potatoes and small cauliflower florets in a giant mixing bowl. Add the oil, salt, pepper, garlic powder, paprika, and oregano and toss everything to coat. Every vegetable needs a light coat of oil, so add a little more if needed. Tip the vegetables onto the unlined baking sheet. Spread them in an even layer and turn the potatoes cut-side down. Roast for 40 minutes, stirring halfway through, until tender and bronzed on the edges.

Transfer the tofu to the parchment-lined baking sheet and roast, stirring halfway through, for 25 to 30 minutes until the edges are golden.

CONTINUED

Winter Bowls with Green Tahini, continued

FOR THE GREENS

1 tablespoon extra-virgin olive oil

1 tablespoon fresh lemon juice

Big pinch of salt and pepper

5 ounces / 140 g spring mix greens

1 cup / 185 g cooked and cooled quinoa

3 green onions, trimmed and thinly sliced

⅓ cup / 40 g toasted pistachios, chopped

Feta or goat cheese

Serves 4

To the bowl you used for the tofu, add the olive oil, lemon juice, 2 spoonfuls of green tahini, and a pinch of salt and pepper and stir to mix. Add the greens, quinoa, and green onions and toss to coat. This will be the base of your bowls.

Assemble the bowls with the greens mixture, a portion of roasted vegetables, and a scoop of tofu. Add a drizzle of green tahini sauce, a pile of pickled onions, pistachios, and crumbled cheese.

CHANGE IT UP

A marinated and grilled flank steak or chicken are excellent substitutes for the tofu; just double the marinade. This makes a crowd-pleasing dinner, and folks can make their bowls to their preference.

Skipping the cheese also makes these bowls dairy free and vegan.

CHAPTER 5

SOUPS, STEWS + MAKE AHEAD

198   Everyday Lentil Soup

201   Italian Farro Soup

202   Turkey Chili

203   Curried Chickpea Bowls

207   Carrot + Red Lentil Dal

208   Sweet Potato Taco Stew

211   Gingered Butternut Soup

212   Cauliflower Tikka Masala

217   Roasted Butternut Orzo Bake

219   Smoky Cauliflower Enchiladas

223   Mixed Mushroom Bolognese

226   Hawaiian Chicken Meatball Bowls

229   Sloppy Jane Sweet Potato Boats

232   Summer Tortellini Salad

233   Corn Chip Chicken Nuggets with Yogurt Ranch

Everyday Lentil Soup

This soup is almost entirely pantry staples, comes together quickly, is stewy enough that it is easy for the kids to eat with bread, and it reheats beautifully for lunch the following day (which any soup maker will tell you is when the soup shines). I call for two kinds of lentils not to complicate things but because the red lentils break down and add heartiness to the broth while the green lentils hold shape and give the soup some texture.

Add a seeded, chopped jalapeño along with the other vegetables if you'd like more of a kick. I call for turmeric but a mild curry powder is a great substitute. Skip it if those aren't your favorite flavors. Unsweetened coconut cream is called for, but a large pat of butter will do the trick for a creamy finish.

1 yellow onion

1 large carrot, peeled

1 medium sweet potato, peeled

2 stalks of celery, trimmed

3 tablespoons / 35 ml olive oil

3 cloves of garlic, minced

1 teaspoon sea salt

½ teaspoon freshly ground pepper

1 teaspoon Italian herbs

¼ teaspoon red pepper flakes, to taste

½ cup / 100 g green or Puy lentils

½ cup / 100 g split red lentils

4 cups / 960 ml vegetable or chicken broth

1 (14.5-ounce / 411 g) can crushed tomatoes

½ teaspoon turmeric or mild curry powder, optional

¼ cup / 60 ml coconut cream or full-fat coconut milk

3 loosely packed cups / 65 g roughly chopped kale

Juice of 1 small lemon

½ cup / 15 g chopped parsley

Grated Parmesan or plain Greek yogurt, optional

Toasted baguette

Serves 4

Finely chop the onion, carrot, sweet potato, and celery. In a large Dutch oven over medium heat, warm the olive oil. Add all the vegetables, including the garlic, to the warm pot. Add the sea salt and sauté until the onions are translucent, about 5 to 8 minutes. Stir in the pepper, Italian herbs, red pepper, and both lentils. Add the broth and tomatoes and stir. Bring the soup up to a gentle boil, then turn the heat to a low simmer, leave the cover ajar, and cook for 30 minutes until everything is tender but not mushy.

Using an immersion blender, give the soup a few pulses just to give it some texture, but nothing near a puree. You want the texture of the vegetables to come through while giving the broth a bit more body. Same can be done by blending one-third of the soup in a standard blender. Turn off the heat. Stir in the turmeric, coconut cream, kale, and lemon juice and cook until the greens start to just soften into the soup, about 2 minutes. Season with more salt and pepper, to taste. Add more broth as needed for your desired thickness.

Serve each bowl with a sprinkle of parsley and Parmesan or yogurt. Best served with a crusty baguette on the side.

SOUP TEXTURE IS A PERSONAL PREFERENCE
I like my lentil soups on the looser side, but know it is always easier to add liquid than to take it away. Use more broth to reheat leftovers as it thickens with time.

Italian Farro Soup

This is a great soup to prep ahead during the busy days of fall, when you come home and need to have dinner already made. If you aren't using the parboiled, quick-cooking farro, you'll need to add ten more minutes to that simmering step.

2 tablespoons extra-virgin olive oil

1 yellow onion, chopped

1 medium fennel bulb, cored and chopped

2 carrots, thinly sliced

2 stalks of celery, diced

3 cloves garlic, diced

1 teaspoon sea salt, to taste

1 teaspoon freshly ground pepper

½ pound / 225 g hot Italian sausage, optional

1 tablespoon tomato paste

1 teaspoon Italian seasoning

Pinch of red pepper flakes

1 (14-ounce / 400 g) can crushed tomatoes (fire-roasted, if possible)

1 quart / 960 ml chicken or vegetable stock

5 ounces / 140 g quick-cooking farro

1 (14-ounce / 400 g) can cannellini or white beans

1 tablespoon balsamic vinegar

2 cups / 75 g chopped Swiss chard or kale

Grated Parmesan

Chopped flat-leaf parsley

Serves 6

Heat the oil in a large Dutch oven over medium heat. Add the onion, fennel, carrots, and celery and sauté for 5 minutes until the onions are translucent. Add the garlic, salt, and pepper and sauté another minute until fragrant. If you are using the sausage, push the meat out of the casing and brown it, breaking it up into small pieces with a wooden spoon.

Add the tomato paste, Italian seasoning, and pepper flakes and stir to mix. Add the tomatoes, stock, farro, and beans and simmer gently, cover ajar, until the grains are cooked through, 15 to 20 minutes.

Turn off the heat and stir in the balsamic vinegar and greens. Give them a minute or two to wilt into the soup. Taste and adjust for seasoning.

Serve in bowls with lots of fresh Parmesan and a sprinkle of fresh herbs.

CHANGE IT UP

Vegetarian: We usually add the sausage, but the soup has plenty of texture and filling ingredients without it. Add a second can of beans if you'd like your vegetarian version to be thicker.

MAKE AHEAD

The whole soup is great made in advance; just add the fresh greens when you're ready to eat so they retain some vibrant color. The soup will keep for a week in the fridge, and can be frozen for months.

Turkey Chili

We live in a neighborhood connected to three other neighborhoods, and it really shines for Halloween. It is festive and very walkable and bustling in the best way. When we are the starter home for trick-or-treating, I make two big pots of chili: one vegetarian, and this one. All the fixings and a tray of tater tots on the side. It is not spicy as written, so add a spoonful of hot sauce or adobo sauce from a can of chipotles if you want a welcome kick. The smaller the pieces of vegetable the better here, so budget some time for prep.

2 tablespoons avocado or olive oil

1 pound / 450 g ground turkey

Sea salt and freshly ground pepper

1 yellow onion, diced

1 bell pepper, diced

1 jalapeño, partially seeded and minced

3 cloves of garlic, minced

3 packed cups / 220 g tiny cubes of butternut squash

1 teaspoon sea salt, to taste

½ teaspoon freshly ground pepper

2 tablespoons tomato paste

2 teaspoons cocoa powder

1 teaspoon light brown sugar

3 tablespoons chili powder

2 teaspoons cumin

2 teaspoons smoked paprika

Pinch of cayenne

1 (28-ounce / 828 ml) can crushed tomatoes (fire-roasted, if possible)

3 cups / 710 ml vegetable or chicken stock

1 (15-ounce / 425 g) can black beans, drained

1 (15.5-ounce / 439 g) can kidney beans, drained

Sour cream

Shredded cheese

Avocado

Cilantro

Serves 6

Heat the oil in a large pot or Dutch oven over medium heat. Add the ground turkey, a big pinch of salt and pepper, and break it up with the back of a spoon. Cook it until browned, about 4 minutes. Remove from the pot and set aside.

Add another drizzle of oil, then add the onion, bell pepper, jalapeño, garlic, squash, and salt and pepper. Sauté for 8 to 10 minutes until the onions and peppers are tender. Add the browned turkey back into the pot. Add the tomato paste, cocoa powder, sugar, chili powder, cumin, smoked paprika, and cayenne and cook for 1 minute. Add the tomatoes, stock, and beans and stir everything to mix. Bring the mixture to a simmer, turn the heat to low, put the cover on ajar, and cook for 30 to 45 minutes, stirring occasionally, until the squash is completely tender. Add more broth if needed to loosen. Taste for seasoning.

Top with all the toppings!

MAKE AHEAD
Chili holds well, so you can make the chili entirely, store in the fridge for up to 5 days, or keep it frozen for months.

Curried Chickpea Bowls

This recipe borrows generously from Thai and Indian cuisines but makes no attempt at being authentic. Both Thai and Indian curries involve different spices, levels of heat, what liquids are used for the broth, etc., and we love elements of both. Each time I make this, I vary it a bit, but this is a good starting place. There are a plethora of curry paste recipes online, but I usually use store-bought to keep this doable for a weeknight dinner.

The raita, which adds a delightful freshness, is best made the day of, but everything else can be made in advance.

1 small yellow onion, chopped

3 cloves garlic

1 small shallot

2-inch / 5 cm nub of ginger, peeled

1 tablespoon coconut oil

2 tablespoons yellow curry paste

1½ teaspoons sea salt, divided

½ teaspoon freshly ground pepper

1 small head cauliflower, broken into small florets

1 pound / 450 g baby Yukon gold potatoes, quartered

1 bell pepper, chopped

2 cups / 475 ml vegetable or chicken broth

Dash of fish sauce

1 tablespoon honey

1 teaspoon curry powder

1 (13-ounce / 368 g) can crushed tomatoes

1 (14-ounce / 400 ml) can coconut cream

1 (14-ounce / 400 g) can chickpeas, drained

Juice of 1 lime

In a food processor, pulse the onion, garlic, shallot, and ginger a few times until everything is uniformly minced.

In a large Dutch oven, heat the oil over medium heat. Once warm, add the curry paste and toast it for 30 seconds. Add the pulsed aromatic vegetables, half of the salt, the pepper and give it all a stir. Sauté for 3 to 4 minutes until tender. Stir in the cauliflower, potatoes, bell pepper, broth, and fish sauce and bring it to a simmer. Put the cover on and cook for 12 minutes until the potatoes are tender. Add the remaining salt, honey, curry powder, tomatoes, coconut cream, and chickpeas and stir to mix. Turn the heat to low, cover ajar, and simmer the curry for 20 minutes for the flavors to blend. Turn off the heat and stir in the lime juice. Taste for seasoning. Add more broth or coconut milk if you prefer yours thinner.

CONTINUED

Curried Chickpea Bowls, continued

FOR THE CHUNKY RAITA

1 English cucumber

¼ teaspoon cumin

½ teaspoon sea salt

1 large clove garlic, grated

½ cup / 112 g plain yogurt

Zest of 1 lime

¾ cup / 15 g minced cilantro

Steamed white rice

Naan

Toasted cashews, chopped

Cilantro

Serves 4–6

While the curry simmers, make your raita. Halve the cucumber lengthwise and scoop out the seeds. Chop it into a small dice. In a mixing bowl, combine the cumin, salt, garlic, yogurt, and lime zest and stir to mix. Add the cucumbers and cilantro and mix. If it is all a bit thick, add a squeeze of lime juice. Set aside in the fridge until ready to serve.

Serve the bowls with rice, a scoop of the curry, some raita, naan, and toasted cashews and cilantro for garnish.

CHANGE IT UP

If you want to add chicken here, brown 1 pound / 450 g of cubed chicken breasts or thighs in the pot after you toast the curry paste and then continue on as written. You will want to add another 1 cup / 240 ml of broth or coconut milk so things stay saucy with the extra ingredient.

Carrot + Red Lentil Dal

Soups and stews can be a tough sell in my house to anyone besides me, but this one seems to be a crowd-pleaser with my kids. Maybe it's the naan on the side that I forbid going into their mouths without some dal on it? Dal (dhal, daal) is an Indian dish, a soup or stew typically made with split pulses or lentils. It is traditionally heavily spiced, but I go easy here to keep it more kid friendly. We add plain yogurt, toasted coconut, and cilantro for garnish, and you cannot skip the rice and naan. The dal keeps in an airtight container in the fridge for a week-ish and can be frozen for months. Use two chiles if you want more kick.

2 tablespoons coconut oil or ghee

3 cloves of garlic

3-inch / 7.5 cm nub of fresh ginger

1 jalapeño or serrano pepper, partially seeded, minced

1 yellow onion, finely chopped

1 teaspoon sea salt

½ teaspoon pepper

1½ teaspoons coriander

1 teaspoon turmeric

1 teaspoon curry powder

1 teaspoon cumin seeds

1 teaspoon coconut sugar or light brown sugar

1¼ cups / 195 g split red lentils

¼ cup / 60 ml water

1 quart / 960 ml low sodium vegetable stock

3 medium carrots

1 (13.5-ounce / 400 ml) can coconut milk

2 giant handfuls of baby spinach, roughly chopped

2 limes, to finish

Cooked rice

Plain yogurt

Cilantro

Flaked coconut, lightly toasted

Quick Pickled Onions (page 289), optional

Serves 6

In a large pot or Dutch oven, heat the coconut oil over medium heat. Grate the garlic, ginger, and jalapeño into the pan and sauté for just a minute until fragrant. Add the onion, half the salt, and pepper and sauté until translucent, about 2 to 3 minutes. Add the coriander, turmeric, curry powder, cumin, and coconut sugar and stir to mix. Add the lentils, water, broth, and remaining salt, and bring it to a boil, then down to a simmer. Leave the cover on ajar and let everything cook for about 20 minutes.

While it cooks, coarsely grate your carrots. Add them to the pot along with the coconut milk. Simmer until everything is tender and stewy, another 10-ish minutes. Turn off the heat and stir in the spinach and squeeze in the juice of the limes. Adjust the seasoning to taste. It probably needs salt; soup loves salt.

Arrange bowls with rice, a portion of the dal, and garnish with yogurt and cilantro. I like a little crunch from toasted coconut and pickled onions, but it can absolutely go without.

Sweet Potato Taco Stew

Think tortilla soup, but with more to it. Does it look very much like the Turkey Chili (page 202) without the turkey? Yes, yes it does, but it is different! For the evenings when you're hustling between work and the rest of your life, this is a warm welcome home.

The polenta helps thicken the broth, but by all means skip it if it is not something you have on hand. And be generous with your garnishes; they really do make this shine.

3 tablespoons / 45 ml avocado oil, divided

1 small yellow onion, diced

1 jalapeño, partially seeded, minced

1 pound / 450 g cubed chicken breasts

1 quart / 960 ml chicken or vegetable broth

2 heaping cups / 350 g peeled, diced sweet potato (1 medium)

1 bell pepper, diced

3 cloves garlic, minced

1 teaspoon sea salt

2 cups / 140 g shredded green cabbage

1 teaspoon chili powder

1 teaspoon paprika

1 teaspoon garlic powder

1 teaspoon cumin

1 (28-ounce / 800 g) can tomatoes

3 tablespoons / 45 g polenta

1 (13.5-ounce / 400 g) can (1½ cups) black beans, drained

1 cup / 165 g corn kernels, fresh or frozen

1 lime

Corn chips

Sour cream

Avocado

Cotija

Limes

Serves 4–6

Heat half of the oil in a large Dutch oven over medium heat. Add the onion, jalapeño, and chicken and sauté for 5 minutes. Add a splash of the broth, turn the heat to low, and cook for about 10 minutes, until the chicken is cooked through. Remove the chicken to the bowl of a stand mixer to cool completely, then run it with the paddle attachment for a minute to shred the chicken completely. This can also be done in a bowl and shredded with two forks. Set aside.

In the pot, heat the remaining oil. Add the sweet potatoes, bell pepper, garlic, and salt and sauté until the potatoes start to become tender, about 5 minutes. Stir in the cabbage, chili powder, paprika, garlic powder, and cumin. Add the tomatoes, breaking up with the back of a spoon if whole, broth, and polenta and bring the soup to a simmer. Turn the heat to low, stir in the beans and shredded chicken, put the lid ajar, and simmer the soup for 20 minutes until the potatoes soften. Turn off the heat, stir in the corn, the juice of the lime, and let it cool down. Season to taste.

Serve warm with generous garnishes.

CHANGE IT UP
Vegetarian: I have written it with the chicken involved, but you can replace it with a second can of beans.

MAKE AHEAD
This freezes wonderfully! Let the soup cool completely, then transfer it to ziplock bags and freeze flat for easy storage.

Gingered Butternut Soup

My dear friend and neighbor Katie taught me about the bones of this soup, and the hot tip of smooshing an already pureed soup through a strainer to make the soup velvety smooth. I typically don't suggest an extra step and dirty dish unless I think it makes a difference, and this one does. Less like baby food and more like you're eating at a nice restaurant!

The pear here is for natural sweetness; it's a background flavor that makes sense in the final product, but an apple is a great substitute. The soup will keep for up to ten days in the fridge or can be frozen for months.

1 medium butternut squash (about 2 pounds / 900 g)

Olive oil

½ of a medium yellow onion, sliced

1-inch / 2.5 cm piece of ginger, grated

3 cloves garlic, roughly chopped

1 teaspoon sea salt

Freshly ground pepper

Pinch of cinnamon

½ teaspoon Aleppo pepper or chili powder

2 Bartlett pears, chopped

1 tablespoon maple syrup

1 quart / 960 ml chicken or vegetable stock

1 tablespoon salted butter

4 ounces / 113 g crème fraîche or ½ cup / 120 ml coconut milk

Croutons (page 290)

2 green onions, sliced

Freshly ground black pepper

Serves 4

Preheat the oven to 400°F / 200°C and line a baking sheet with parchment paper. Split the butternut lengthwise, rub it with olive oil, and roast for 40 minutes until caramelized and tender. Once cool to the touch, discard the seeds and scoop out the flesh of the squash. You will have about 3 cups / 680 g.

Heat a generous drizzle of olive oil in a Dutch oven over medium heat. Add the onion, ginger, garlic, salt, and freshly ground pepper and cook until translucent, stirring occasionally, about 8 minutes. Add the roasted squash, cinnamon, Aleppo pepper, pears, maple syrup, and stock and simmer everything for 15 minutes. Use an immersion blender or transfer the contents to a high-speed blender and puree until completely smooth. Push the soup through a fine-mesh sieve with a silicone spatula to get the soup through the holes, and back into the pot to keep warm. Stir in the butter and creme fraiche.

Season to taste and top with croutons, green onions, and black pepper.

CHANGE IT UP
Dairy free: You can keep this dairy free with the coconut milk versus creme fraiche option and thin it to taste.

Cauliflower Tikka Masala

This is the one for a chilly day, when a kitchen that smells of warm spices is the exact kind of cozy you crave. This is Hugh's most requested meal, the rich and flavorful sauce over one of our favorite vegetables. He's a quick sell on anything saucy over rice. Sure, it's a good number of spices, but I'll bet you have most of them already, and I've found that even if I'm missing one, the others make up for it. Have your vegetables prepped and you'll be surprised how quickly this all comes together.

2 tablespoons yellow curry powder

1½ teaspoons cumin

1 teaspoon paprika

1 teaspoon turmeric

1 tablespoon coriander

¼ teaspoon cinnamon or allspice

¼–½ teaspoon red pepper flakes

1 teaspoon sea salt

1 medium head cauliflower (about 2 pounds / 980 g), broken into small florets

3 tablespoons / 45 ml avocado oil, divided

1 medium yellow onion, diced

5 cloves garlic, grated

1 tablespoon grated fresh ginger

6 ounces / 170 g tomato paste

1 cup / 240 ml low sodium vegetable stock

1 (14-ounce / 400 ml) can coconut milk

Zest and juice of 1 small lemon

Cooked rice (basmati or brown)

½ cup / 75 g salted, toasted cashews, chopped

Small bunch cilantro, chopped

Plain yogurt or vegan alternative

Naan

Serves 4

Preheat the oven to 425°F / 220°C.

In a small bowl, mix together the curry, cumin, paprika, turmeric, coriander, cinnamon/allspice, red pepper flakes, and salt.

On a rimmed baking sheet, add the cauliflower florets, drizzle with 2 tablespoons of the avocado oil, and toss with about a third of the spice mix. Transfer to the oven and roast for 30 minutes until just browned and tender.

Meanwhile, make your sauce. In a large Dutch oven, heat the remaining oil over medium heat. When the oil is shimmering, add the onion and cook until golden, about 4 minutes. Add the garlic and ginger and cook until fragrant, another minute. Add the remaining spice blend, stir, and let the spices toast for an additional 2 minutes. Stir in the tomato paste. Slowly pour in the stock and coconut milk and bring the sauce to a low boil. Once boiling, turn the heat down to medium and allow it to simmer for 5 minutes, until the sauce has thickened and coats the back of a spoon. Use an immersion blender or transfer the sauce to a blender to puree the sauce until smooth.

Transfer the sauce back to the pot, add the cauliflower, lemon zest, and lemon juice, and stir gently to combine. Add more broth to loosen things as necessary.

To serve, fill bowls with a generous scoop of rice, the tikka, toasted cashews, cilantro, yogurt, and naan.

CHANGE IT UP
Vegan: To keep this completely vegan, top with a plain coconut-based yogurt.

Roasted Butternut Orzo Bake

Hands down my favorite meal to deliver. With a little bit of heat from the jalapeño against the natural sweetness of the squash, and topped with a crispy panko topping, it is an elevated version of . . . a casserole. That word doesn't do it justice! We like orzo here because it's different and bakes up easily, but you can get away with a shell pasta or short rigatoni (mezzi rigatoni).

4 cups / 900 g (1-inch / 2.5 cm) cubed butternut squash, about 1 medium squash

2 tablespoons extra-virgin olive oil

1 teaspoon paprika

½ teaspoon sea salt

¼ teaspoon freshly ground pepper

FOR THE PESTO

2 cloves garlic, peeled

Zest and juice of 1 small lemon

1 jalapeño, partially seeded and chopped

2 cups / 40 g packed green herbs (any combination of parsley, cilantro, chives and/or basil)

½ teaspoon sea salt

¼ teaspoon freshly ground pepper

¼ cup / 30 g toasted pistachio nuts + more for garnish

⅓ cup / 80 ml extra-virgin olive oil

¼ cup / 25 g grated Parmesan

Preheat the oven to 400°F / 200°C.

On a rimmed baking sheet, combine the butternut squash, olive oil, paprika, salt, and pepper and toss to coat. Roast in the oven for 25 to 30 minutes, until golden and tender. Set aside.

Meanwhile, make the pistachio pesto. In a food processor or high-speed blender, pulse the garlic, lemon zest, lemon juice, and jalapeño until well chopped. Add the herbs, salt, pepper, and pistachios. Pulse again. With the motor going, drizzle in the oil and Parmesan until desired texture is reached (I like mine a little rough). Set aside until ready to use.

Make the orzo. Heat a 12-inch / 30 cm ovenproof skillet over medium heat. Add the olive oil. Once warm, add the onion, shallots, salt, and pepper. Sauté until the onions are translucent, about 3 minutes. Add the orzo and stir to combine, until the orzo is coated in oil. Pour in the wine and cook until half of the wine is absorbed, about 2 minutes. Turn the heat down to low and stir in the stock, butter, lemon zest, and kale. Bring the mixture to a gentle simmer. Cover the skillet transfer to the oven, and bake for 15 minutes.

Meanwhile, in a small bowl, combine the panko, half of the Parmesan, and olive oil and stir to combine.

CONTINUED

Roasted Butternut Orzo Bake, continued

FOR THE ORZO

1 tablespoon extra-virgin olive oil

½ of a yellow onion, thinly sliced

2 shallots, peeled and thinly sliced

½ teaspoon sea salt

¼ teaspoon freshly ground pepper

1 cup orzo (about 8 ounces / 225 g)

½ cup / 120 ml dry white wine

2 cups / 475 ml chicken or vegetable stock

2 tablespoons unsalted butter

1 tablespoon lemon zest

2 cups / 35 g kale, roughly chopped

½ cup / 85 g panko

½ cup / 50 g grated Parmesan cheese, divided

1 tablespoon extra-virgin olive oil

1 cup / 40 g grated fontina cheese, divided

Serves 4–6

Carefully remove the skillet from the oven and stir in half of the pistachio pesto (reserving the rest for serving). Stir in the roasted squash, half of the fontina, and the rest of the Parmesan. Sprinkle the remaining fontina over the top, along with the Parmesan panko. Transfer it back to the oven, uncovered, and bake for an additional 10 minutes. Turn the oven to broil, and broil until the top is just golden, another 1 to 2 minutes.

Allow the skillet to cool for 10 minutes before serving. Serve portions with a bit of extra pesto, a sprinkle of pistachios, and a fresh green salad.

CHANGE IT UP

If you are looking to add more protein, add 8 ounces / 225 g browned Italian sausage or crispy cooked bacon pieces when you add the squash.

MAKE AHEAD

Both the pesto and the roasted squash can be made in advance.

FREEZER TIP

Make it through the first covered baking step all the way to topping with remaining fontina and Parmesan panko. Cool to room temperature, cover tightly with foil, then freeze. From the freezer, let it sit out as you preheat the oven, bake it for 30 minutes, then broil until the top is just golden, another 1 to 2 minutes.

Smoky Cauliflower Enchiladas

Making enchilada sauce is easier than you think. A little sauté and a blend, that's it. It will keep for about five days in the fridge, so it can be made in advance. That said, your time-saver tip here is to use a prepared sauce; we like Frontera and Siete brands, red over green!

We use corn tortillas, but any small to medium tortilla works great. Corn tortillas don't roll as easily as wheat, but I like that they're small and gluten free. Traditionally, the tortillas are fried before rolling to help hold their shape, but I don't want the extra oil and don't mind that the tortillas break down a bit.

1 small cauliflower, broken into small florets, about 4 cups / 430 g

2 tablespoons avocado oil

1½ tablespoons taco seasoning

FOR THE ENCHILADA SAUCE

3 tablespoons /45 ml avocado oil

2 cloves garlic, chopped

3 tablespoons / 25 g flour (all-purpose, whole wheat, gluten free, all work)

2 teaspoons chili powder

1 teaspoon cumin

¼ teaspoon dried oregano

3 tablespoons / 45 g tomato paste

2 cups / 480 ml vegetable broth

2 teaspoons apple cider vinegar

¼ teaspoon sea salt

Freshly ground pepper

Preheat the oven to 400°F / 200°C. Collect the cauliflower on a baking sheet, drizzle it with the oil and taco seasoning, and toss to coat. Spread in an even layer and roast for 25 to 30 minutes, stirring halfway through, while you prepare the rest of your bits.

If you are making your sauce from scratch, make that while the cauliflower roasts. In a skillet over medium heat, warm the avocado oil. Add the garlic and sauté until fragrant, just a minute. Add the flour and dry spices and cook until toasty, 1 to 2 minutes. Whisk in the tomato paste to combine. While you continue whisking, slowly add the broth until smooth and combined. Simmer the sauce for 5 minutes to thicken. Turn off the heat. Stir in the vinegar, salt, and pepper.

In a large mixing bowl, combine the red peppers, drained beans, sundried tomatoes, smoked paprika, and all the bits from the cauliflower pan. Add the lime juice, cilantro, green chiles, and half of the cheese. Stir to mix.

Heat the tortillas over a gas stovetop or in a cast-iron pan, until just toasty and pliable. Create an assembly line.

CONTINUED

Smoky Cauliflower Enchiladas, continued

1 (6-ounce / 170 g) jar roasted red peppers, drained and chopped

1 (13-ounce / 368 g) can pinto beans, drained

¼ cup / 80 g sundried tomatoes, minced

1 teaspoon smoked paprika

Juice of 1 lime

½ cup / 10 g chopped cilantro + more for serving

4 ounces / 113 g mild green chiles

2½ cups / 285 g shredded Mexican-blend cheese, divided

10 small corn or wheat tortillas

Quick Pickled Onions (page 289)

Sour cream

Avocado

Lime wedges

Serves 6

Pour about ½ cup / 120 ml of enchilada sauce into the bottom of a 13-by-9-inch / 33-by-22 cm (or similar) baking dish. Put a heaping ¼ cup / 60 ml of filling down the center of each tortilla and roll. Place it seam-side down and repeat with the remaining tortillas and filling. Pour enchilada sauce over the tops of the enchiladas and sprinkle the remaining cheese over the top. Cover them loosely with foil and bake for 15 minutes. Remove the foil, turn the heat up to 450°F / 230°C and bake another 10 minutes until the cheese just browns on top.

Out of the oven, sprinkle with fresh cilantro. Serve them with pickled onions, sour cream, avocado, and wedges of fresh lime.

MAKE AHEAD
To freeze, fully assemble the enchiladas, wrap them tightly in foil, and freeze. Pull the tray out of the freezer while you preheat the oven, and add 20 to 25 minutes to the covered baking time.

Mixed Mushroom Bolognese

The goal here is to get all the vegetables chopped super small, so I urge you to pulse in a food processor if you have one. I'm not one to try to pull a fast one by suggesting that a vegetarian riff on a traditional meat dish is anything besides that, but the minced veggies here really help you get a great texture for serving. They also help with picky kids! I like this one with polenta or pappardelle pasta, my family prefers it on English muffins with some cheese melted over the top, Sloppy Joe–style. This Bolognese will keep for up to five days in the fridge or can be portioned and frozen for months.

We typically cook polenta 3:1, water to polenta, and finish it with a big nub of butter, salt, and glug of milk. I always stop cooking when it's on the looser side, as it firms up as it rests, much like oatmeal.

2 tablespoons olive oil

1 small yellow onion, minced

2 ribs celery, minced

1 small fennel bulb, cored and minced

1 large carrot, minced

1 teaspoon sea salt + more to taste

½ teaspoon freshly ground pepper

2 tablespoons salted butter

4 cloves garlic, minced

16 ounces / 450 g mixed mushrooms (any kind but shiitake), wiped clean and finely chopped

2 tablespoons tomato paste

½ cup / 120 ml red wine

½ cup / 100 g cooked lentils

½ cup / 120 ml whole milk

1 (28-ounce / 800 g) can crushed tomatoes (fire-roasted, if possible)

1 teaspoon dried Italian seasoning

2 teaspoons fennel seeds, crushed

Red pepper flakes, to taste

3 tablespoons / 40 g creme fraiche

Noodles or polenta

Grated Parmesan

Fresh flat-leaf parsley, chopped

Serves 6

Warm the olive oil in a large Dutch oven over medium heat. Once hot, add the onion, celery, fennel, carrot, salt, and pepper. Cook until tender and reduced, stirring occasionally, about 8 minutes. Remove the vegetables to a bowl while you cook the mushrooms.

To the pot, add the butter, garlic, mushrooms, and big pinches of salt and pepper, and sauté again. Cook, stirring occasionally, for about 10 minutes, until the water has cooked out of the mushrooms and they have reduced down to one-third of their original volume. Add the onion mixture back in, along with another pinch of salt and pepper, the tomato paste, and wine and cook another 5 minutes to reduce the wine. Stir in the lentils, milk, crushed tomatoes, Italian seasoning, fennel seeds, and red pepper flakes to taste and stir to combine. Gently simmer, with the cover ajar, for 30 to 40 minutes until the lentils are tender. Stir in the creme fraiche, if using, and adjust seasonings to taste.

Serve over pasta or polenta with fresh Parm and parsley.

CHANGE IT UP

We've done a half-meat version with success—simply add ½ pound / 225 g of ground turkey or beef in with the mushrooms to brown and forget the lentils (or leave them, honestly, it's pretty forgiving).

Vegan: Replace the milk with a plain nondairy creamer, the butter and creme fraiche with a nondairy butter, and skip the cheese to keep it vegan.

Hawaiian Chicken Meatball Bowls

This meal is an example of "micro prepping," where I can get most of the way to dinner in other small windows of my day. If you're halfway there by the time dinner rolls around, you're less likely to talk yourself out of cooking and order takeout. This system also helps enormously if you're entertaining, so you can enjoy your company instead of being in the kitchen the whole time. Prepare the meatball mixture and the slaw in advance to get you most of the way. Or you can get even further if you cook the rice and the meatballs with the sauce and pineapple, and simply reheat them at mealtime.

Depending on where you purchase ground chicken, sometimes it can be very wet. If your meatball mixture seems really tacky, add a little more panko and let it rest, uncovered, in the fridge to dry it out further. The easiest brand of Hawaiian or island teriyaki sauce to find is by Soy Vay; it's usually near the other Asian condiments or BBQ sauces, which is where you will also find coconut aminos, a sweet and savory condiment similar to soy sauce.

FOR THE MEATBALLS

1 large egg

⅓ cup / 55 g panko

1 tablespoon coconut aminos

2 teaspoons soy sauce or tamari

2 teaspoons toasted sesame oil

3 cloves garlic, grated

3-inch / 7.5 cm nub of ginger, grated

¼ of a red onion, minced

½ cup / 10 g chopped cilantro

½ teaspoon sea salt

Freshly ground pepper

1 pound / 450 g ground chicken, dark meat

FOR THE COCONUT RICE

1¼ cups / 125 g short-grain white rice, rinsed

1 cup / 240 ml water

1 cup / 240 ml coconut milk

Sea salt

Pepper

Zest of 1 lime

For the meatballs, in a medium bowl, combine the egg, panko, coconut aminos, soy sauce, sesame oil, garlic, ginger, onion, and cilantro and a few big pinches of salt and pepper. Stir to combine. Add the ground chicken and mix to combine. Set aside to rest for 15 minutes. This can be done a day in advance and kept covered in the refrigerator. If the mixture is too wet to roll, add another ¼ cup / 40 g panko.

Start your rice. Combine the rinsed rice, water, coconut milk, salt, pepper, and lime zest together. Stir to mix. Bring the rice up to a boil, then down to a simmer. Cover and cook for 18 to 20 minutes until cooked and tender. Set aside.

The meatballs can be cooked on the stove top or in the oven.

For the stove-top method, heat a generous drizzle of oil in a skillet over medium heat. Form the meatballs into small balls and sear them in the oil. You may need to do this in two batches, depending on the size of your skillet. Shake them around to brown on all sides. Once they are mostly cooked through, add the pineapple pieces and give them a sear, turn the heat to low, and add the teriyaki sauce and coconut milk. Shake the pan around again for the sauce to mix and to coat all the meatballs in sauce. Cover the pan and let it simmer for 10 minutes to warm through.

Coconut oil or avocado oil, for cooking

2 cups / 350 g fresh pineapple pieces, cut small

1 cup / 240 ml store-bought Hawaiian-style teriyaki sauce

½ cup / 120 ml coconut milk

FOR THE SLAW

3 tablespoons / 45 ml mayonnaise

1 tablespoon toasted sesame oil

1 tablespoon agave nectar

1 tablespoon apple cider vinegar

Juice of 1 lime

Sea salt

Freshly ground pepper

1 small bundle Tuscan kale, de-ribbed and cut into ribbons

½ head green cabbage, cored and finely sliced

1 bundle green onions, white and green parts thinly sliced

3 tablespoons / 30 g toasted sesame seeds

Toasted coconut

Chopped cilantro

Chili crisp

Avocado

Serves 4–6

To bake, preheat the oven to 425°F / 220°C. Form the meatballs into small balls, arrange them on an oiled, rimmed baking sheet, and bake for 15 minutes. Turn on the broiler, add the pineapple to the baking sheet, and give it all 1 more minute under the broiler. Transfer the contents to a skillet to finish in the sauce as described in the preceding paragraph.

While it simmers, in a mixing bowl, whisk up the mayo, sesame oil, agave, vinegar, lime juice, and a big pinch of salt and pepper. Add the kale, cabbage, and green onions and toss to coat. Add the sesame seeds and toss again.

Serve the bowls with a scoop of rice, meatballs, slaw, and garnishes of choice.

Sloppy Jane Sweet Potato Boats

A satisfying baked sweet potato, a warm and well-spiced turkey mixture, and a bright and snappy slaw to balance everything. A tender baked potato stands in for the classic English muffin—a raft for all the fillings—so we have more fiber and vegetables involved here. Little kids may still request the classic "boat," and for ease, I wouldn't decline.

4 medium sweet potatoes

1 tablespoon avocado oil

FOR THE SLAW

½ a red onion, thinly sliced

Zest and juice of 2 limes

1 teaspoon cane sugar

1 teaspoon sea salt

½ cup / 10 g chopped cilantro

1 tablespoon avocado oil

2 tablespoons mayonnaise or Veganaise

2 tablespoons red wine vinegar

1 small jalapeño, seeded and sliced thin

1 small head green cabbage shredded (5 cups / 350 g)

½ cup / 60 g toasted pepitas

Preheat the oven to 400°F / 200°C. Clean and prick your sweet potatoes all over with a fork. Rub the skins lightly with oil. Bake them for 45 to 55 minutes or until completely cooked through (you should be able to pierce through to the center easily). Prepare the rest while your potatoes bake.

For the slaw, in a large bowl, soak your onion in lime zest and juice; this helps mellow out the onion flavor. Let it sit for 5 minutes, then add the sugar, salt, cilantro, oil, mayo, vinegar, and jalapeño and stir to combine. Add the cabbage and toss to dress. Top with the pepitas and pop the bowl in the fridge until ready to serve.

CONTINUED

Sloppy Jane Sweet Potato Boats, continued

FOR THE SLOPPY JANES

1 tablespoon avocado oil

1 small yellow onion, finely chopped

1 red bell pepper, finely chopped

½ teaspoon sea salt, to taste

3 cloves garlic, minced

2 tablespoons tomato paste

1 pound / 450 g ground turkey

1 teaspoon dried oregano

1 teaspoon smoked paprika

2 teaspoons chili powder

2 tablespoons balsamic vinegar

2 tablespoons coconut aminos

1 tablespoon Dijon mustard

1 cup / 240 ml tomato sauce

½-1 cup / 120-240 ml chicken stock, divided

2 tablespoons chopped chives

Avocado

Serves 4

To make the Sloppy Jane mix, heat the oil in a large Dutch oven over medium heat. Once hot, add the onion, bell pepper, and salt and cook until tender, about 4 minutes. Add the garlic and tomato paste and cook another minute. Add the turkey, breaking it up well until browned, about 4 minutes. Add the oregano, paprika, and chili powder and sauté again to combine. Add the balsamic, coconut aminos, Dijon, tomato sauce, and ½ cup / 120 ml of the stock and stir well. Bring the mixture to a gentle simmer and cook for 10 minutes. Stir in the chives. Add stock to taste.

To assemble, split open your warm sweet potatoes and season them with salt and pepper. Add a scoop of the turkey mixture, slaw, and avocado for garnish.

MAKE AHEAD

The Sloppy Jane mix can be done days in advance and kept covered in the fridge.

CHANGE IT UP

Vegan: Sub in 8 ounces / 245 g minced mushrooms, 1 cup / 200 g cooked lentils, and ½ cup / 65 g chopped walnuts, and you have a great vegan alternative.

Summer Tortellini Salad

If you are looking for a dish for new parents, a potluck, or desk lunch, this is a great one. It also makes a great meal to pack for a plane ride because all the vegetables and chickpeas get even better as they marinate in the dressing. The ingredient list looks long-ish, but they are mostly pantry goods.

FOR THE VINAIGRETTE

½ teaspoons dried oregano

1 tablespoon grated Parmesan

1 clove garlic, grated

Red pepper flakes, to taste

1 teaspoon Dijon mustard

3 tablespoons / 45 ml champagne vinegar

1 tablespoon liquid from the pepperoncini jar

1 tablespoon fresh lemon juice

½ teaspoon sea salt

1 teaspoon agave or honey

⅓ cup / 80 ml olive oil

8 ounces / 225 g cherry tomatoes, halved

¼ of a red onion, sliced thin and rinsed

⅓ cup / 80 g Castelvetrano olives, pitted and torn

2 Persian cucumbers, seeded and diced

⅓ cup / 45 g pepperoncini, drained

½ cup / 130 g chickpeas, rinsed and drained

½ cup / 120 g marinated artichoke hearts, chopped

3 ounces / 85 g dry salami, cut in small cubes, optional

10 ounces / 285 g cheese tortellini, cooked and rinsed

2 cups / 40 g baby arugula

1 bunch basil, chopped

Toasted pine nuts

Shaved Parmesan or ricotta salata

Serves 4

In a large mixing bowl, whisk up all the vinaigrette ingredients.

To the bowl, add the tomatoes, onion, olives, cucumbers, pepperoncini, chickpeas, artichoke hearts, salami, and the cooked tortellini. Toss to coat. Chill for 30 minutes to an hour if you have the time, but don't worry about it if you don't. Add the arugula, basil, a sprinkle of cheese, and toss again.

Garnish with the pine nuts and more cheese and serve!

MAKE AHEAD
This can be made a day in advance. Wait to add your greens until you're ready to serve so they stay crisp.

CHANGE IT UP
Vegetarian: The salami is optional—plenty going on without it.

Corn Chip Chicken Nuggets with Yogurt Ranch

For better or worse, life with young children is full of crispy chicken in many forms. It has even resurfaced my own affection for crackly crusted chicken—paired with sauces, and maybe even tossed into a salad? Yes, please.

Double this recipe to reheat or freeze for another time, as these are an easy hit with the kiddos. I cook them all the way through, store in the fridge, then reheat them in a toaster oven or an air fryer for eight to ten minutes. This recipe is for the nuggets and a simple ranch, but for an adult dinner, add these crispy nuggets to the Taco Salad (page 175).

If you think ahead, an overnight soak in the buttermilk marinade is ideal.

When I say "corn chips" I mean something resembling Fritos, not tortilla chips. Trader Joe's and Pipcorn make our favorites.

1 cup / 240 ml buttermilk or plain yogurt

1 teaspoon smoked paprika

½ teaspoon garlic powder

1 teaspoon each sea salt and pepper

1¼ pounds / 565 g chicken breast

½ cup / 60 g all-purpose or tapioca flour

2 large eggs

2 tablespoons milk

1 (12-ounce / 340 g) bag corn chips

1 teaspoon onion powder

1 teaspoon garlic powder

1 teaspoon dried dill

Avocado oil cooking spray, for cooking

In a large mixing bowl, combine the buttermilk, paprika, garlic powder, salt, and pepper and stir. Pound the chicken down to a 1-inch / 2.5 cm thickness and cut it into ½-inch- / 1.25 cm-wide fingers or nuggets. Add the chicken pieces to the bowl and stir. Set aside to marinate while you prepare your other ingredients. Marinate ideally overnight, up to a day in advance.

Create an assembly line with three shallow bowls. In one, put your flour or tapioca flour. In another shallow bowl, whisk up your eggs and milk. In a food processor, pulse your chips into small crumbs. Put the crumbs in the last shallow bowl, and stir in the onion powder, garlic powder, and dried dill.

Preheat the oven to 400°F / 200°C. Set a cooling rack over a parchment paper–lined, rimmed baking sheet.

CONTINUED

Corn Chip Chicken Nuggets with Yogurt Ranch, continued

FOR THE YOGURT RANCH

1 clove garlic, chopped

⅓ cup / 80 ml mayonnaise

½ cup / 112 g plain yogurt

1 teaspoon garlic powder

½ teaspoon paprika

½ teaspoon dried dill

Zest of 1 lemon + 3 tablespoons / 45 ml juice

2 teaspoons white wine vinegar

½ teaspoon sea salt

½ teaspoon freshly ground pepper

1 teaspoon Dijon mustard

Handful of parsley

Handful of fresh chives

Serves 4

Move through your assembly line. Let the excess buttermilk drip off the chicken, flop the pieces around in the flour, then the egg wash, and let the excess drip off. In batches, tumble the chicken in the seasoned crumbs, pressing them in, and place them on the prepared rack. Repeat with all the chicken pieces. Spray them with cooking spray. Bake for 16 to 20 minutes, flipping the chicken pieces halfway through, until cooked through and golden.

While the chicken bakes, make your ranch. In a blender or food processor, pulse the garlic to mince. Add the mayo, yogurt, garlic powder, paprika, dried dill, lemon zest and juice, vinegar, salt, pepper, and Dijon and pulse again. Add the parsley and chives, and pulse again until they are small flecks. Taste for seasoning.

Serve your nuggets with ranch.

The chicken will keep for 2 to 3 days in the fridge to reheat as needed, or frozen for up to 3 months.

CHAPTER 6

TREATS

238   Strawberry Rhubarb Crumble Bars

243   Honey Almond Fudge Bar

244   Chocolate-Covered Cashew Cookie Dough Bites

247   Vegan Coconut Caramel

248   Almond Flour Double Chocolate Cookies

251   Browned Butter Oatmeal Chocolate Chip Cookies

252   Mixed Berry Crisp

254   Key Lime Pie

257   Cherry Almond Bundt

258   Memaw's Peach Cake

263   Our One-Bowl Carrot Cake

267   Gingersnap Pumpkin Tart

268   Birthday Cupcakes

271   Peppermint Brownies with Ganache

277   Dairy-Free Chocolate Peanut Butter Budinos

Strawberry Rhubarb Crumble Bars

A spring favorite here, jammy and fragrant and definitely passable as a breakfast pastry.

If strawberries are not in season, swap out your fruit: peaches in the late summer, or an apple and caramel layer in the fall! Rhubarb has a short window but can be replaced with another cup of any berry should it be unavailable.

FOR THE FILLING

1 tablespoon orange juice

1 pound / 450 g strawberries, hulled and finely chopped

2 stalks rhubarb, finely chopped (1 cup / 120 g)

⅓ cup / 72 g light brown sugar or coconut sugar

¼ teaspoon cinnamon

¼ teaspoon ground ginger

2 teaspoons lemon zest

2 tablespoons cornstarch or arrowroot powder

FOR THE CRUST AND CRUMBLE

1 cup / 90 g old-fashioned oats

1 cup / 120 g all-purpose flour or gluten-free 1:1 flour

¾ cup / 84 g slivered almonds, divided

½ cup / 113 g coconut oil, as a solid (4 ounces / 113 g cold butter or vegan butter works too)

⅓ cup / 72 g light brown sugar or coconut sugar

1 teaspoon vanilla extract

½ teaspoon baking powder

½ teaspoon cinnamon

½ teaspoon sea salt

2 tablespoons cold water

Makes 9 bars

Preheat the oven to 350°F / 180°C. Line an 8-inch / 20 cm baking pan with a parchment paper sling, and grease with cooking spray or butter.

In a heavy pot over medium heat, combine the orange juice, strawberries, rhubarb, sugar, cinnamon, ginger, and lemon zest. You may need a sprinkle more sugar if your berries aren't tops. Simmer the fruit, uncovered, until it has cooked down and looks a bit jammy, about 10 minutes. Mix the cornstarch or arrowroot with a splash of orange juice until smooth, and stir that into the berry mixture. Simmer another 10 minutes. Turn off the heat and let it cool.

For the crust and crumble, in a food processor, pulse together the oats, flour, ½ cup / 56 g of the almonds, coconut oil, sugar, vanilla, baking powder, cinnamon, and salt. Pulse just a few times. We still want to see flecks of oats; it should look crumbly. Add the cold water and pulse until the dough will press together and stick when you press it between your fingers.

Transfer half of the crust mixture to the prepared pan and press it down into an even layer. Bake for 15 minutes until the top is just toasted. Allow the crust to cool completely.

CONTINUED

Strawberry Rhubarb Crumble Bars, continued

Once cooled, distribute the fruit filling evenly over the surface. Stir the remaining ¼ cup / 28 g slivered almonds and another sprinkle of sugar into the remaining crumble/crust mixture and sprinkle it over the top. Return to the oven and cook for an additional 30 minutes until golden brown.

Allow the bars to cool completely. They're easier to cut if you refrigerate them for an hour. Using the edges of the parchment, remove the bars carefully. Transfer to a cutting board and cut into squares with a sharp knife. You can cut them smaller, but they are delicate and may fall apart more easily.

Store the bars covered in the fridge for 3 to 5 days.

CHANGE IT UP

We make these with a vegan butter or coconut oil (sometimes a mix) to keep them dairy free, but real-deal butter works great as well.

Honey Almond Fudge Bar

Years ago, I fell in love with this chocolate bar called Honey Mamas. It is basically a honey-sweetened fudge made with coconut oil and almonds. I made a crunchier knock-off version after I found myself hiding the expensive bars from my family in an attempt to hoard my special treat.

Because coconut oil is solid when chilled, the bars do need to stay refrigerated to hold shape, but they keep well there for months. These can take on aromatics or add-ins. Try a dash of peppermint extract, espresso powder, or toasted coconut flakes.

2 ounces / 60 g dark chocolate, finely chopped

½ cup / 70 g whole almonds

⅓ cup / 30 g cocoa powder (natural or Dutch process) or raw cacao powder + more for dusting

Pinch of sea salt

⅓ cup plus 1 tablespoon / 95 ml honey

⅓ cup / 80 ml coconut oil

1 teaspoon vanilla extract

½ cup / 15 g crisp rice cereal

Makes 10 small bars

Line a standard (1 pound / 8.5-inch / 21 mm) loaf pan with a sling of parchment paper for easy removal. Sprinkle the chopped chocolate along the bottom of the pan.

In a food processor, combine the almonds, cocoa powder, and sea salt. Pulse the mixture until it resembles coarse sand, about ten times. You want some crunchy bits of almonds.

In a saucepan, combine the honey and coconut oil and bring it to a simmer. Stir to mix for 1 minute. Turn off the heat and stir in the vanilla extract.

Add the almond mixture and the rice cereal into the wet mixture and stir to combine. Any extra add-ins would go in here. Transfer the mixture to the prepared pan, press down and smooth the top, and put it in the fridge to chill for at least an hour.

Once cooled, dust the top with cocoa. Cut the fudge into squares or rectangles and keep covered in the fridge for up to 2 months.

Chocolate-Covered Cashew Cookie Dough Bites

I have seen a hundred versions of date nut balls, energy balls, and nut butter balls, all different ratios of similar ingredients. Some with crispy rice or crunchy nut butters or oats inside. Cashews give us the creamiest texture, and all this chocolate makes them taste decadent. Keep them in the fridge for a sweet snack, and they will last for weeks.

If your dates seem a little dry, soak them in warm water for fifteen minutes and drain before proceeding with the recipe.

1 heaping cup / 113 g raw cashew pieces

2 tablespoons coconut oil

3 tablespoons / 45 ml maple syrup

1 teaspoon vanilla extract

½ teaspoon sea salt

6 Medjool dates (a few extra if using a smaller variety like Deglet Noor)

2 tablespoons coconut flour

⅓ cup / 58 g semisweet mini chocolate chips

4 ounces / 113 g dark chocolate, chopped

2 teaspoons coconut oil

Makes 14 pieces

Into a food processor, dump the cashews and process until smooth and creamy, about 2 to 3 minutes. Add the coconut oil, maple syrup, vanilla, salt, dates, and coconut flour and run again. It will form into a ball of sorts, which is fine. Add the chocolate chips and pulse a dozen or so times to break up the chocolate.

Form the mixture into small balls and collect them on a parchment paper–lined plate or container. Chill in the fridge for at least 1 hour.

To make the coating, melt the chopped chocolate and coconut oil together until smooth. Dip the chilled balls into the chocolate and roll them around to coat. Or use a fork and drizzle some chocolate over the top of each ball for a lighter coating. Place them on the parchment-lined plate and repeat. Pop the plate into the fridge for the chocolate to set.

The balls can be stored in the fridge for a few weeks.

CHANGE IT UP

Skip the chocolate and add freeze-dried strawberries to the cashew mixture.

Replace half the cashews with hazelnuts and add 2 tablespoons cocoa powder for a Nutella vibe.

Vegan Coconut Caramel

Drizzle this smooth and creamy dairy-free caramel over an ice cream sundae or Cinnamon-Apple Baked Oatmeal (page 24), or use it as a dip for apple slices. I love the whiskey caramel from the Gjelina cookbook, and inspired by that smoky background liquor flavor, I've suggested bourbon as an option here. Makes more sense for an ice cream topping than a breakfast oatmeal for kids in that case, but! You're the cook.

This is thinner just off the stove than traditional caramel, but it will firm up in the fridge. The best serving temperature will vary based on application. Bring it to room temperature for dipping, or heat it gently for drizzling.

⅔ cup / 145 g light brown sugar

1 (13.5-ounce / 400 g) can coconut cream

2 tablespoons maple syrup

2 tablespoons cashew butter

1 teaspoon vanilla extract

Sea salt

2 teaspoons bourbon, optional

Makes 1½ cups / 350 ml

In a heavy-bottomed pot, combine the sugar and coconut cream. Bring it to a gentle simmer over medium heat, stirring often, for about 20 minutes until the sugar has dissolved and the mixture has reduced slightly. Off the heat, whisk in the maple syrup, cashew butter, vanilla, a big pinch of salt, and bourbon, if using, until completely smooth, about 2 minutes.

Keep the caramel covered at room temperature for a few days or stored in the fridge for 2 to 3 weeks.

Almond Flour Double Chocolate Cookies

There is an almond meal cookie in our first cookbook that is one of the top three recipes made from that book, if metrics are taken by shared Instagram photos, that is. They are gluten free and light while still feeling like a treat: rich but delicate, sweet but not cloying. Just the right amount of decadence. I brainstormed how I could make a sister cookie to those winners, and the only way to make them better is more chocolate, so here we are.

I prefer almond flour (typically blanched) to almond meal, but either will work in equal measure; there will just be a slight texture difference.

1 large egg, room temperature

⅓ cup / 80 g coconut oil, warmed to a liquid

2 tablespoons smooth nut butter

½ teaspoon almond extract or vanilla extract

1 teaspoon instant coffee or finely ground coffee

1 cup / 112 g almond flour or meal

2 tablespoons tapioca starch

¼ cup / 21 g Dutch-processed cocoa powder

½ cup / 110 g light brown sugar or muscovado

¼ cup / 50 g sugar

½ teaspoon sea salt

Scant ½ teaspoon baking soda

½ teaspoon baking powder

3½ ounces / 100 g semisweet chocolate, finely chopped

Makes 14–16 cookies

In a stand mixer with paddle attachment or large mixing bowl, combine the egg, warmed coconut oil, nut butter, almond extract, and coffee. Mix well until the mixture is smooth and glossy.

In a separate bowl, combine the almond flour, tapioca starch, cocoa powder, light brown sugar, sugar, salt, baking soda, and baking powder. Whisk to combine. Add the dry ingredients to the wet and stir to combine. Fold in the chopped chocolate, using your hands if needed, to incorporate. Put the mixture in the fridge for 30 minutes or up to overnight to chill.

Preheat the oven to 350°F / 180°C. Line two baking sheets with parchment paper.

With a small scoop or your hands, form the dough into small (roughly 2-tablespoon-size) balls and arrange them with space to spread on the baking sheets. Bake for 9 minutes, rotating the sheets halfway through, and smacking the baking sheet on the counter out of the oven. Let them cool completely. Just believe me, the warm ones will fall apart in your hands. They must be cool to hold shape!

The cookies will keep, covered, at room temperature, for 3 days.

Browned Butter Oatmeal Chocolate Chip Cookies

I make a lot of our treats and snacks with almond meal and dairy alternatives and hidden produce, but when it comes to a chocolate chip cookie, you need a back-pocket recipe for a classic version. Make the dough in advance, and bake off the cookies just after dinner so they are nice and warm and your house smells like a dream. I make these for new moms and teachers, or to bookend a sturdy ice cream sandwich.

9 tablespoons / 130 g salted butter

2 teaspoons finely ground coffee or instant coffee

½ cup / 100 g sugar

½ cup / 110 g light brown sugar

1 large egg, room temperature

1 egg yolk, room temperature

1 teaspoon vanilla extract

½ teaspoon almond extract

½ cup / 45 g old-fashioned oats

1½ cups / 180 g unbleached all-purpose flour

¼ teaspoon baking soda

½ teaspoon baking powder

½ teaspoon sea salt

¾ cup / 128 g semisweet chocolate chips (or 4 ounces / 113 g chopped dark chocolate)

Flaky salt, for finishing

Makes 14

In a small saucepan over medium heat, melt the butter. Swirl it around. Warm it enough to be fragrant, just golden, and a little nutty smelling, about 10 minutes. Off the heat, stir in the coffee grounds. Let it cool down and transfer it to a stand mixer with the paddle attachment or a large mixing bowl. Let it cool completely.

Add the sugar and brown sugar and mix until well incorporated. Add the egg, egg yolk, vanilla and almond extracts and mix again. Add the oats, flour, baking soda, baking powder, and salt and mix until the flours are just mixed in. Add the chocolate and mix one more time. Put the mixture in the fridge for 30 to 60 minutes to chill while you line two rimmed baking sheets with parchment paper and preheat the oven to 350°F / 180°C.

Make balls of about 3 tablespoons' worth of dough and space them on your baking sheets. Sprinkle the tops with flaky salt. Bake for 10 minutes, rotating the pans halfway through, then slam the pans down on the counter when you remove them. They will look underdone and I promise that's alright; they'll set as they cool.

Cookies will keep, covered, for 2 days, but are a dream about 20 minutes out of the oven.

CHANGE IT UP
I often sub chopped dark chocolate bars in place of the chocolate chips to make these look a little fancier. Bake them straight on the baking sheet for a slightly crisper bottom crust. If you use a dairy-free butter, skip the browning step and just melt it.

MAKE AHEAD
Roll balls of raw dough and freeze them for a later use. To bake, bring them out while you preheat the oven, and add 3 minutes to the baking time.

Mixed Berry Crisp

Even if you don't consider yourself a baker, this one is foolproof. Especially served a la mode, this is our favorite summer dessert and a complete crowd-pleaser for any eater. I always serve a crisp à la mode but will sneak a bowlful for breakfast with some plain yogurt.

FOR THE FILLING

6 cups / 24 ounces mixed berries (any large strawberries, chopped)

2 tablespoons arrowroot or cornstarch (or all-purpose flour)

¼ cup / 50 g sugar

¼ teaspoon freshly grated nutmeg

Pinch of salt

1 tablespoon fresh lemon juice

FOR THE CRISP

½ cup / 113 g unsalted butter, coconut oil, or plant-based butter alternative, room temperature

½ cup / 28 g finely shredded coconut

1 cup / 90 g sliced almonds

⅓ cup / 72 g light brown sugar or coconut sugar, packed

¼ cup / 50 g sugar

1 cup / 85 g almond meal, all-purpose flour, or gluten-free 1:1 flour

1 cup / 90 g quick oats

½ teaspoon baking powder

1 teaspoon vanilla extract

½ teaspoon almond extract

½ teaspoon sea salt

Ice cream, for serving

Serves 6

Preheat the oven to 350°F / 180°C. Butter or oil a 2-quart / 9-inch / 23 cm ovenproof baking dish.

Collect all the berries in a large mixing bowl. Sprinkle the arrowroot or cornstarch over the top, along with the sugar, grated nutmeg, salt, and lemon juice. Stir everything to mix. Transfer to your baking dish.

Combine the butter or coconut oil, coconut, sliced almonds, both sugars, almond meal, oats, baking powder, vanilla and almond extracts, and salt. Using your clean hands, work the butter or oil into the dry ingredients until the mixture looks sandy and combined. This can also be done in a food processor.

Spread the mixture over the top of the berries and press it down gently. Bake the crisp in the bottom third of the oven for 35 minutes until the edges are bubbling juices and the top is golden. If using frozen fruit, add 10 minutes to the baking time.

Remove to rest for at least 20 minutes for the crisp to settle. Serve warm with ice cream.

CHANGE IT UP

This works with stone fruits too. Just use the same weight of peeled and chopped peaches and add a dash of almond extract. If you want to do an apple swap, double the lemon juice and add cinnamon to both the filling and topping. For frozen fruit, add a tablespoon more of cornstarch/arrowroot. If shredded coconut is not your favorite, replace it with more oats or nuts.

Nut free: The almond products may be replaced with the same yield of all-purpose flour or gluten-free 1:1 flour if nuts need to be avoided. This makes for a more biscuity topping.

Dairy free: Sub the butter for a dairy-free alternative or coconut oil.

Key Lime Pie

For my dad, who took me on date nights to the Chart House as a teen—where we always finished our bottomless salad bar dinner with a warm chocolate lava cake or key lime pie that had twice as much whipping cream as custard. The guy who always says he "doesn't want dessert" but eats most of it. This has not been made more "esoteric," Dad, to your request. Love you.

6 ounces / 170 g graham crackers (about 2 cups of crumbs)

2 tablespoons cane sugar

7 tablespoons / 100 g salted butter, room temperature

Zest of 2 limes

4 egg yolks

Juice of 4 large limes (½ cup / 120 ml)

1 (14-ounce / 414 ml) can sweetened condensed milk

1 cup / 240 ml heavy cream

½ cup / 56 g powdered sugar

½ teaspoon vanilla extract

Salt

Zest and thin slices of 1 lime, for garnish

1 (9-inch / 23 cm) pie

Preheat the oven to 350°F / 180°C.

In a food processor, pulse the grahams into a fine crumb. Add the sugar and butter and pulse a dozen more times to get a damp-looking, sandy mixture. Press the mixture into the bottom and up the sides of a 9-inch / 23 cm pie pan. You can use the bottom of a measuring cup or damp fingers to press it.

Bake for 12 minutes. Remove to cool completely, but leave the oven on. Just out of the oven, press the mixture down again to pack it down a little more.

In a mixing bowl, combine the lime zest and egg yolks and whisk well to combine and get some air up in there. Add the lime juice and condensed milk and whisk again until well mixed. Pour the mixture into the cooled crust and bake another 13 minutes to set. Not brown!

Cool the pie to room temperature, then leave it to chill in the fridge for at least 2 hours. All of this can be made 2 to 3 days in advance.

Whip your cold heavy cream to fluffy peaks. Add the powdered sugar, vanilla, and a pinch of salt and whip it again to combine.

Onto your cold pie, pile the whipping cream, leaving a ½-inch / 1.25 cm border around the edge of the pie. Zest a lime over the top. The pie should be chilled for another hour at this point so it slices more cleanly.

Cut the pie into slices and serve with a thin slice of lime for garnish.

Cherry Almond Bundt

Perfect with tea or coffee, or with a scoop of vanilla bean ice cream. The almond paste adds a rich and unique almond flavor and is a favored pairing with cherries, which grow on the same genus of tree. I find almond paste in well-stocked baking sections or online. It is sweetened and *not* the same as almond butter.

A standard Bundt pan is somewhere around 10 to 12 cups / 2.3 to 2.8 L. This will fill the pan about halfway and rise slightly from there. If you have a unique size, adjust your baking time and check the center for doneness.

½ cup / 113 g salted butter, room temperature + more for greasing the pan

1 cup / 200 g sugar

7 ounces / 200 g almond paste

4 large eggs

½ cup / 120 ml avocado oil

1 teaspoon almond extract

1 teaspoon vanilla extract

2 tablespoons lemon juice

½ teaspoon sea salt

1 cup / 96 g almond flour

1¼ cups / 150 g all-purpose flour + more for dusting the pan

1¼ teaspoons baking powder

¼ teaspoon baking soda

1½ heaping cups / 200 g pitted, chopped cherries

Powdered sugar

Makes 1 (12-cup / 2.8 l) cake

Preheat the oven to 350°F / 180°C and butter and flour a Bundt pan.

In a stand mixer with the paddle attachment, combine the butter, sugar, and almond paste and mix until completely combined, about 2 minutes. With the mixer running, add the eggs, one at a time, the oil, almond and vanilla extracts, lemon juice, and salt and mix again to combine.

Add both flours, baking powder, and baking soda and fold everything together to just combine. Add the cherries and give it all a few more folds. Transfer the batter to the prepared pan and smooth the top. Bake on the middle rack for 52 to 55 minutes until the cake is cooked through with a toothpick test.

Remove to cool completely. It needs to settle for cleanest removal.

Once cool, gently remove the cake. Sprinkle some powdered sugar on top.

The cake is best within 2 to 3 days and should be wrapped tightly in plastic wrap. It can be wrapped and frozen for a few months.

DRESS IT UP
Make a glaze with 1½ cups / 170 g powdered sugar, 1 tablespoon plain yogurt, 1 tablespoon orange juice, a drop of vanilla, and a pinch of salt. Stir until completely smooth. Drizzle over the top of the cooled cake.

Memaw's Peach Cake

She did not fancy herself a cook, but my memaw had a peach tree and she loved dessert. Her way was a Duncan Hines yellow cake mix, tons of chopped juicy summer peaches from the tree, and cinnamon sugar over the top. The cake is revisited every summer, because food memories are magic, especially when you miss someone. Below is the version that will live in this cookbook and make me think of her.

I prefer the texture when the peaches are all in small pieces, but it looks more dramatic with larger wedges—you choose. I don't usually peel the peaches but you can for a more polished texture. It's really worth hanging on to this recipe until you can get the juice-down-your-arm, eat-it-over-the-sink, late-summer golden peaches.

½ cup / 113 g salted butter, room temperature + more for greasing the pan

2 tablespoons extra-virgin olive oil, or coconut or avocado oil

¾ cup / 150 g sugar + more for sprinkling

2 large eggs, room temperature

1 teaspoon vanilla extract

½ teaspoon almond extract

⅓ cup / 80 g buttermilk, room temperature

1¼ cups / 150 g all-purpose flour or cake flour

½ cup / 48 g almond flour

⅓ cup / 52 g cornmeal

½ teaspoon ground cinnamon

Grate of fresh nutmeg

1¼ teaspoons baking powder

½ teaspoon baking soda

Pinch of sea salt

3 medium peaches (1 pound / 450 g), pitted and chopped small

Whipped cream

Serves 6–8

Preheat the oven to 350°F / 180°C. Grease a 10-inch / 25 cm cast iron or 9-inch / 23 cm square pan and set aside.

In a stand mixer with the paddle attachment, mix the butter, oil, and sugar together until combined and fluffy, about 2 minutes. Add the eggs and beat another few minutes until incorporated. Add the vanilla and almond extracts and buttermilk and mix again. At this point, the butter and such may separate a bit, but don't worry about it.

Add the flour, almond flour, cornmeal, cinnamon, nutmeg, baking powder, baking soda, and pinch of salt. Mix again until just combined. The batter will be thick, similar to the texture of cornbread. Fold in the chopped peaches (it will look like a lot but just trust it!).

Tip the batter into the prepared pan, smooth out the batter, and sprinkle a layer of sugar over the top. Bake on the middle rack for 40 to 50 minutes, until a toothpick test in the center comes out clean. Allow it to rest for an hour before cutting it in slices.

The cake will last, covered, in the fridge for up to 3 days. Because of the fresh fruit, it will only last at room temperature for 1 to 2 days.

CHANGE IT UP

Gluten free: This cake works great with a swap of a gluten-free 1:1 flour, such as Bob's Red Mill or King Arthur; increase the baking powder to 1½ teaspoons for a bit more lift.

Our One-Bowl Carrot Cake

People have opinions about carrot cake. I am calling this "ours" because I think you can make it "yours" based on your own carrot cake preferences. This one leans "snacking cake": great for any time of day and less like a traditional layer cake for a special occasion. I like lots of goodies in mine, hold the raisins, not too sweet, and there must be frosting, but not a super heavy one. Some of you are very pro-raisins or anti-nuts and I assure you, this cake can handle some futzing. It's forgiving—my favorite kind of baked good.

2 large eggs

½ cup / 120 ml coconut oil, warmed, or avocado oil + more for greasing the pan

¼ cup / 60 ml maple syrup

⅔ cup / 135 g sugar

1 teaspoon vanilla extract

1 tablespoon orange zest

¾ teaspoon cinnamon

¼ teaspoon ground ginger

A few grates of fresh nutmeg

8 ounces / 225 g crushed pineapple

1½ packed cups / 165 g finely grated carrots

⅓ cup / 40 g walnuts, well chopped

½ packed cup / 30 g shredded coconut

1 cup / 112 g oat flour

1 cup / 135 g super fine brown rice flour

¼ cup / 35 g tapioca flour

1¼ teaspoons baking powder

½ teaspoon baking soda

½ teaspoon sea salt

Preheat the oven to 360°F / 185°C and line a 9-inch / 23 cm square pan with parchment paper and grease that.

In a large mixing bowl, whisk together the eggs, oil, maple syrup, sugar, vanilla, orange zest, cinnamon, ginger, and nutmeg. Add the pineapple, carrots, walnuts, and coconut and stir. Add the oat flour, rice flour, tapioca flour, baking powder, baking soda, and salt and stir everything to combine. Pour it into the prepared pan and bake it on the middle rack for 26 to 28 minutes until a toothpick test in the middle comes out clean. It will set more as it cools.

CONTINUED

Our One-Bowl Carrot Cake, continued

FOR THE FROSTING

8 ounces / 225 g cream cheese, room temperature

6 tablespoons / 85 g unsalted butter, room temperature

2 teaspoons orange zest

2 teaspoons orange juice

½ cup / 120 ml maple syrup

½ cup / 50 g powdered sugar

1 teaspoon vanilla extract

½ teaspoon sea salt

Toasted walnuts or shredded coconut, optional

Serves 6-8

While the cake bakes, make your frosting. In a stand mixer, mix your cream cheese and butter until combined and smooth, about 2 minutes. While the machine is running, add the orange zest and juice, maple syrup, powdered sugar, vanilla, and salt and mix until well combined. It will be thinner than a traditional frosting.

When the cake is completely cool, spread the frosting on top. Garnish with toasted walnuts or coconut if you're feeling fancy.

Store at room temperature for a day, or covered in the fridge for up to 5 days.

CHANGE IT UP

Dairy free: The cake itself is dairy free. If you prefer your glaze to be dairy free as well, Kite Hill makes a nondairy cream cheese product that will work in the same ratio, and there are vegan butters (Miyoko's is our fave!) as well.

All-purpose flour swap: 1¾ cups / 210 g for the oat, rice, and tapioca flours.

Gluten free take 2: You can also swap in 2¼ cups / 270 g of King Arthur Measure for Measure or Bob's Red Mill 1:1 gluten-free flour in place of the oat, rice, and tapioca. These can replace all or one of the flours in equal measure.

Gingersnap Pumpkin Tart

A snappy crust of gingersnap cookies offers both texture and that beloved fall spice. It buoys this creamy pumpkin filling, which is lighter than cheesecake but still luxurious enough to cap off a delicious meal.

12 ounces / 340 g gingersnap cookies

2 tablespoons light brown sugar

½ cup / 45 g old-fashioned oats

Pinch sea salt

⅓ cup / 75 g salted butter, vegan butter, or coconut oil, room temperature

8 ounces / 225 g whipped cream cheese, room temperature

2 teaspoons pumpkin pie spice

1 teaspoon vanilla extract

1 cup / 227 g pumpkin puree

2 large eggs, room temperature

⅔ cup / 160 ml maple syrup

⅓ cup / 72 g light brown sugar

Pinch of salt

Whipped cream or whipped coconut cream, for serving

Cinnamon, for serving

Crystallized ginger, optional

Makes 1 (10-inch / 25 cm) tart

Preheat the oven to 350°F / 180°C.

In a food processor, combine the gingersnaps, sugar, oats, and pinch of salt and pulse until sandy. Add the butter or oil and pulse a few more times. The mixture should stick together when you press it with your fingers; add a drizzle more oil or butter if it feels dry. Press the mixture evenly into a tart pan, up the sides as well, and bake on the middle rack for 10 minutes. Remove to cool. Use a measuring cup to press the warm crust down again, particularly pressing in the elbows of the tart pan. Turn the oven down to 325°F / 165°C.

While the crust cools, make your filling. In a blender, combine the whipped cream cheese, pie spice, vanilla, pumpkin, eggs, maple syrup, brown sugar, and a generous pinch of salt and whiz to combine. We want it completely smooth, so keep going, you can't hurt it. Pour the mixture into the cooled crust and bake for 25 minutes until just set.

Remove the tart to cool, then chill it in the fridge for a couple of hours before serving. Garnish with lightly sweetened whipped cream, a pinch of cinnamon, and crystallized ginger, if using, sprinkled on top.

CHANGE IT UP

Gluten free: Use gluten-free gingersnaps in the crust.

Dairy free: It works great with a vegan butter and our favorite dairy-free cream cheese, Kite Hill, in place of regular cream cheese. I have made it all the ways and don't find those swaps to make this tart any less fabulous.

Birthday Cupcakes

I do love a boxed cake mix and then making a simple buttercream from scratch for a quick yet upgraded birthday treat. However! With a stocked pantry, these cupcakes are almost as easy. There are few things as darling as a kid with their own candle-adorned birthday cupcake.

Cooking spray

2 large eggs

⅓ cup / 80 g sour cream or yogurt

1 tablespoon vanilla extract

1¼ cups / 300 ml brewed coffee

½ cup / 120 ml avocado or melted coconut oil

½ cup / 40 g cocoa powder

1½ cups / 300 g cane sugar

½ teaspoon sea salt

1¾ cups / 210 g all-purpose or cake flour

1½ teaspoons baking soda

1 teaspoon baking powder

3 ounces / 85 g dark chocolate, well chopped (or ½ cup / 113 g chocolate chips)

FOR THE BUTTERCREAM

1 cup / 225 g salted butter, room temperature

3 cups / 340 g powdered sugar

1 tablespoon sour cream or milk

1 teaspoon vanilla extract

Makes 18 cupcakes

Preheat the oven to 350°F / 180°C. Prepare your pans: Line 18 muffin cups with parchment liners and spray lightly with oil.

Combine the eggs, sour cream, vanilla, coffee, and oil in a bowl, and whisk well to combine. In another bowl, stir together the cocoa powder, sugar, salt, flour, baking soda, baking powder, and chopped chocolate. Fold the wet and dry mixes together until completely incorporated, being careful not to overmix. Let it rest for 5 minutes, then transfer the batter to your prepared pans, filling your cupcake liners three-quarters full.

Bake the cupcakes on the middle rack for 22 to 24 minutes, testing the center with a toothpick to make sure they are cooked through. Cool completely.

While the cupcakes cool, make your buttercream. Put the room temperature butter in a stand mixer with the paddle attachment and mix for a few minutes until fluffy. Add the powdered sugar (in stages to prevent a mess!), sour cream or milk, and vanilla extract and mix again until smooth and fluffy. Add a splash more milk if you need help moving it.

Frost your **cooled** cupcakes and keep them stored at room temperature for up to a day, or covered in the fridge for 3 days.

CHANGE IT UP

I did not call for real vanilla beans in the buttercream, but if you have them, those tiny brown flecks are so pretty! To elevate it further, brown the butter and let it cool to room temperature before making the buttercream. To make it pink and strawberry flavored, use 1 ounce / 28 g of freeze-dried strawberries and whiz them in the mixer first to break them down. For chocolate, incorporate 2 ounces / 57 g melted and cooled semisweet chocolate.

You can also make one 10-by-15-inch / 25-by-38 cm (jelly roll pan) cake or two 8-inch / 20 cm round cakes. Grease the pans and line the bottoms with parchment paper, then dust with cocoa powder and tap out the excess. The baking time will vary, so use a toothpick to test the center for doneness.

Vegan: Replace the eggs with one medium mashed banana and 2 tablespoons flax meal. They will be slightly more dense.

Gluten free: We have had luck with Bob's Red Mill or King Arthur 1:1 gluten-free flour.

Peppermint Brownies with Ganache

These are classic, rich, and hands down my favorite dessert when topped with a scoop of ice cream. We crown them with one more layer of rich chocolate ganache and some crushed peppermint candies (as in candy canes or the red-and-white swirly ones) to take these over the top.

You'll be tempted to cut into them straight out of the oven, but they really need to settle into themselves. Allow them to cool entirely before trying to slice them. A sharp knife, run under warm water and wiped clean between cuts, always helps get clean edges.

5 tablespoons / 70 g salted butter

3½ ounces / 100 g dark or semisweet chocolate, roughly chopped

⅓ cup / 28 g Dutch-processed cocoa powder

½ cup + 1 tablespoon / 113 g sugar

½ cup / 110 g light brown sugar or muscovado sugar

2 large eggs

¼ cup / 60 ml avocado or coconut oil

1 teaspoon vanilla extract

1 teaspoon peppermint extract

½ cup + 1 tablespoon / 62 g unbleached all-purpose flour

½ teaspoon baking powder

¼ teaspoon sea salt

⅓ cup / 85 g semisweet chocolate chips

Preheat the oven to 350°F / 180°C. Line an 8-by-8-inch / 20-by-20 cm square pan with a parchment paper sling, covering the bottom and also providing overhang over the sides for easy removal. Set aside.

In a medium glass bowl over a pot of simmering water, melt the butter. Once melted, add the chopped chocolate and gently stir together until smooth and glossy. Remove from the heat and immediately whisk in the cocoa powder. Set aside to cool.

In a medium mixing bowl, combine the sugar, brown sugar, and eggs. Whisk well to get some good volume in there, at least 2 minutes. Add the oil and vanilla and peppermint extracts. Whisk again. To test, lift your whisk out of the mixture and ensure a thick ribbon streams down. This helps with texture and a good crackly top.

To the egg mixture, slowly mix in the chocolate-and-butter mixture. Whisk well until totally combined with no streaks.

Sift in the flour, baking powder, and salt. Stir gently until just combined. Add the chocolate chips and give it one more stir.

Transfer the batter into your prepared pan and bake on the middle rack for 22 to 24 minutes, until just set in the center (they will continue to set as they cool).

CONTINUED

Peppermint Brownies with Ganache, continued

FOR THE CHOCOLATE GANACHE

3½ ounces / 100 g dark or semisweet chocolate, roughly chopped

2 tablespoons heavy cream or coconut oil

½ teaspoon peppermint extract

⅓ cup / 65 g crushed peppermint candies, optional

Flaky sea salt

Makes 1 (8-by-8-inch / 20-by-20 cm) pan

While they cool, make your ganache. In a microwave-safe bowl, combine the chopped chocolate, cream or coconut oil, and peppermint. Microwave on medium power, in 30-second increments, stirring well each time, until just melted and smooth. (This can also be done in a glass bowl over simmering water.)

Once the brownies are cool, pour the ganache over them. Sprinkle the peppermint candies and flaky salt over the top and let them cool to set (speed this up by placing them in the fridge for 1 hour).

Remove the parchment sling from the pan. Cut the brownies into small squares with a clean, sharp knife.

Brownies will keep covered at room temperature for 3 days.

CHANGE IT UP

If mint is not your favorite, eliminate the extract and add 2 teaspoons finely ground coffee or instant espresso. Or add ⅔ cup / 80 g walnut pieces or crushed up Oreo cookies. Chopped peanut butter cups or a swirl of peanut butter on top is another favorite.

Dairy free: Replace the butter with a vegan alternative or coconut oil. Be sure your dark chocolate does not contain milk solids.

Gluten free: Replace the flour with oat flour and 2 tablespoons of arrowroot powder or a 1:1 gluten-free all-purpose blend.

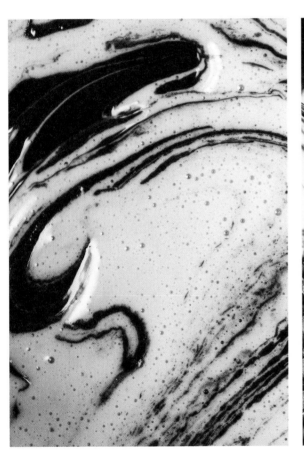

Dairy-Free Chocolate Peanut Butter Budinos

If you grew up on instant chocolate pudding, you'll love this deeper chocolate, super quick, dairy-free alternative. You simply simmer a coconut milk base on the stove, fold in a good-quality chopped chocolate and some other bits, and top it all off with a salty, peanut butter topper. Designed to evoke nostalgia, these little *budinos* are perfect for a weekend treat or a dinner party. Kid and adult approved.

Substitute runny almond butter and roasted, salted almonds in place of the peanuts, if you prefer.

FOR THE PUDDING

1 (13.5-ounce / 400 ml) can full-fat coconut milk

¼ cup / 60 ml maple syrup

⅓ cup / 37 g powdered sugar

2 tablespoons arrowroot

2½ ounces / 70 g dark (semi-sweet) chocolate, roughly chopped + some for garnish

⅓ cup / 28 g Dutch-processed cocoa powder, sifted

½ teaspoon vanilla extract

Pinch of sea salt

FOR THE PEANUT BUTTER LAYER

½ cup / 128 g smooth, salted, runny peanut butter, room temperature

4–6 tablespoons / 60–90 ml water + more as needed

4 tablespoons / 60 ml maple syrup

Whipped coconut cream

Crumbled graham crackers

Chopped roasted and salted peanuts

Serves 4–6 budinos

In a saucepan over medium heat, stir together the coconut milk, maple syrup, powdered sugar, and arrowroot. Whisk to combine, bringing the mixture to a gentle simmer. Once hot, add the chocolate and simmer, whisking occasionally, until the chocolate is melted, about a minute. Add the cocoa powder and whisk again until smooth. Turn off the heat and stir in the vanilla and pinch of salt.

Transfer the mixture into four to six ramekins. Transfer to the fridge to cool for 2 hours or, preferably, overnight.

Whisk the peanut butter, water, and maple syrup until smooth. If your peanut butter seizes, like tahini, stir in more water, 1 tablespoon at a time. We want to get it drizzleable. Once chilled, pour a layer of the peanut butter on top of each pudding and chill again.

When ready to serve, garnish with a dollop of coconut whipped cream, grated chocolate, crushed graham crackers, and a sprinkle of peanuts.

CHAPTER 7

DRESSINGS, CONDIMENTS + BASICS

280   Everyday Pesto

280   Mexican Caesar

281   Green Harissa

282   Salsa Mercado

282   Aji Verde

283   Shallot Date Vinaigrette

283   Green Tahini

286   Another Green Sauce

286   Romesco-ish

287   Gorgonzola Vinaigrette

287   Everything Cashew Sauce

288   Avocado Pepita Sauce

288   Coconut-Peanut Stir-Fry Bowl Sauce

289   Double Mustard Maple Dressing

289   Quick Pickled Onions

290   Salad Crunchies

290   Corn Tortillas

292   Day-Ahead Pizza Dough

Everyday Pesto

A classic! And used for so much more than just pasta. If you can't find fragrant basil, a combination of parsley and cilantro makes for a lovely winter pesto. You can swap in different nuts and seeds accordingly; I like cilantro and pepita or smoked almonds and parsley. They all make excellent dipping sauces with grilled chicken and vegetable skewers or hearty pasta sauces. If you use it for warm pasta dishes, incorporate some of the pasta water (and a nub of butter!) to help the pesto spread.

2 cloves garlic

3 tablespoons / 20 g lightly toasted pine nuts

1 teaspoon sea salt

½ teaspoon freshly ground pepper

2 cups / 40 g basil leaves, packed

2 tablespoons fresh lemon juice

½ cup / 120 ml extra-virgin olive oil

¼ cup / 25 g grated Parmesan cheese

Makes 1 cup / 240 ml

In a food processor, combine the garlic, pine nuts, salt, and pepper and pulse a few times to mince. Add the basil, lemon juice, and olive oil and pulse a few more times. Add the Parmesan and pulse again to your desired texture. If it looks dry, add a splash of water. Season to taste.

Transfer to a container with a lid and store in the fridge for up to a week.

Tip for keeping it bright green? Bring a pot of salted water to a boil, and leave a bowl of ice water ready next to it. Blanch the basil leaves for five seconds. No more, no less. Count to five and then transfer to the ice bath to shock them. Drain completely. Is this essential? No. But it does keep it a vibrant green for longer.

WHERE ELSE TO USE THIS?

Jumbo rigatoni pasta and roasted cauliflower

In a veggie sandwich on toasted focaccia, with fresh mozzarella, arugula + summer tomatoes

Thinned with lemon juice to make a salad dressing with kale, white beans, cherry tomatoes, olives + more grated Parm

Flatbread sauce

With toasted crostini and burrata

Mexican Caesar

This is perhaps my favorite recipe in this book. Have I already said that about another recipe? Originally written for the Mexican Brussels (page 125), it is also great on a kale or cabbage slaw, spread on a wrap, or drizzled on any veggie bowl.

We get out of using a traditional Caesar's raw egg yolk by including a dollop of mayo here. It can be Vegenaise or plain, whole Greek yogurt if you'd rather, but either way, this is a bit thinner than a traditional Caesar dressing. I know anchovy scares some of you, so use half, but please don't skip it! I promise it isn't "fishy."

2 cloves garlic, minced

2 small anchovy fillets

2 teaspoons Dijon mustard

Dash of Worcestershire sauce

1 jalapeño, charred (see note)

1 small bunch cilantro, leaves only, roughly chopped

Handful of fresh parsley, roughly chopped

¼ cup / 56 g mayonnaise

¼ cup / 25 g freshly grated Parmesan cheese

¼ teaspoon sea salt, to taste

½ teaspoon freshly ground pepper

3 tablespoons / 45 ml lime juice (about 1 juicy lime)

2 tablespoons white wine vinegar

⅓ cup / 80 ml extra-virgin olive oil

Makes 1 heaping cup / 240 ml

In a blender or food processor, combine the garlic, anchovy, Dijon, Worcestershire, and charred jalapeño. Pulse a few times to chop. Add the cilantro, parsley, mayonnaise, Parmesan, salt, pepper, lime juice, and vinegar, and pulse again. With the motor running, drizzle in the olive oil until combined.

Keep the dressing in a covered container in the fridge for a week or two.

To char the jalapeño, on the stovetop or outdoor grill, turn the heat to medium-high and place the pepper directly on the grates. Use tongs to carefully rotate it every 30 seconds or so until it is covered with char marks, about 4 minutes. To roast the pepper in the oven, bake it at 450°F / 230°C for 15 to 20 minutes. Let it cool to the touch and push the burnt skin off with your hands. I like to partially seed it at this point for a medium level of heat.

Green Harissa

It is punchy and bright and spicy in the best way. Great as is, also excellent with a bit of Vegenaise or mayo to get it closer to Peruvian aji verde (which also tones down the heat). Try it on salmon off the grill, mixed with summer corn, over grain bowls, or painted on roasted, smashed potatoes! You'll find this harissa used in Green Harissa Salmon Skewers with Savory Peach + Cucumber Salad (page 141).

If you like things hot, leave the jalapeño seeds and ribs intact; take out some or all of them to reduce the heat level.

2 cloves garlic, chopped

2 jalapeños, seeded to your heat preference, chopped

1 packed cup / 20 g cilantro

1 packed cup / 20 g flat-leaf parsley

½ cup / 10 g mint leaves

3 tablespoons / 45 ml fresh lemon juice

½ teaspoon cumin

½ teaspoon coriander

½ teaspoon fennel seed

¾ teaspoon sea salt

⅓ cup / 80 ml extra-virgin olive oil

Makes 1 cup / 240 ml

In a food processor or blender, pulse the garlic and jalapeños a few times to mince. Add the cilantro, parsley, mint, lemon juice, cumin, coriander, fennel seed, and salt and pulse again. With the motor going, add the oil and run until it has a chunky/smooth-ish texture. Taste and adjust for seasoning.

The harissa will store in an airtight jar in the fridge for a week.

Salsa Mercado

This will remind you of restaurant salsa—to the point and perfect for dipping. I leave half the seeds in the jalapeño and end up with a crowd-pleasing, medium-heat salsa. Use a hotter pepper, like a serrano, or even two, if you like it really spicy. I'm mostly looking for chip dip or something to juice up an ordinary taco.

2 cloves garlic

¼ small yellow onion, roughly chopped

¼ small red onion, roughly chopped

1 jalapeño, chopped

1 (14-ounce / 400 g) can diced tomatoes (fire-roasted, if available)

2 Roma tomatoes, quartered

2 giant handfuls of cilantro

2–3 tablespoons lime juice (about 1 lime)

½ teaspoon cumin

¼ teaspoon chili powder

1 teaspoon sea salt

Makes 1½ cups / 360 ml

In a food processor, combine the garlic, onions, and jalapeño. Pulse a few times to mince. Add the canned and fresh tomatoes, cilantro, lime juice, cumin, chili powder, and salt. Pulse the processor a dozen times until everything is blended but still a little chunky. Taste for seasoning. Store covered in the fridge for up to a week.

Aji Verde

A Peruvian green sauce. I don't like the tang of regular mayonnaise, so I use Vegenaise here for personal preference. Either works. This is a lot of jalapeño, so I suggest seeding them. Every pepper is different, but you should still get plenty of warmth. A squeeze of honey or agave may not be authentic, but will balance the heat. Use it on tacos, bowls, salmon, or chicken. It's an "everything sauce" for sure.

3 jalapeños, seeded, roughly chopped

1 bundle cilantro

2 cloves garlic, chopped

½ cup / 113 g Vegenaise or mayonnaise

¼ cup / 56 g sour cream

1 tablespoon grated Parmesan cheese

3 tablespoons / 45 ml lime juice

½ teaspoon sea salt

Freshly ground pepper

1 tablespoon extra-virgin olive oil

Makes 1 cup / 240 ml

Put all ingredients in a food processor or blender and whiz until smooth.

CHANGE IT UP
Dairy free: There are a handful of dairy-free sour cream alternatives out there, and a plain coconut yogurt will also work in its place.

Shallot Date Vinaigrette

A text of affection, for me, goes something like "I had this amazing salad with the best dressing and I think you could copy it." That is how we found this incredible dressing: via my friend Katie after dining at a spot called Bells on the California central coast. It's sweet-ish and nuanced and has that umami goodness from the nutritional yeast and Parm. So good!

2 Medjool dates, pitted

2 tablespoons water

2 tablespoons chopped shallots

1 clove garlic, chopped

1 teaspoon Dijon mustard

1 tablespoon lemon juice

¼ cup / 60 ml champagne vinegar

2 teaspoons nutritional yeast

1 tablespoon grated Parmesan cheese

Handful of fresh parsley

Handful of fresh chives

⅔ cup / 160 ml extra-virgin olive oil

1 teaspoon sea salt

½ teaspoon freshly ground pepper

Makes 1 cup / 240 ml

Put all the ingredients in a food processor or blender and blend until smooth. Add water if you want to thin it further. This vinaigrette will last 1 to 2 weeks stored in the fridge.

CHANGE IT UP
We use it as a basic vinaigrette, but I could see it leaning Mediterranean . . . maybe even with a pinch of curry to push it more Indian-ish.

Green Tahini

I love a tahini-based sauce for all the Mediterranean dishes we make around here—bowls, pita sandwiches, falafels, etc. This can all be whisked together by hand if you get your garlic and herbs chopped finely first and then combine everything really well. It will be more textured, not smooth, which is not a bad thing.

1 clove garlic, roughly chopped

½ serrano pepper, seeded, roughly chopped

1 cup / 15 g fresh green herbs, roughly chopped (some combo of basil, parsley, chives, cilantro)

1–2 teaspoons white or yellow miso paste

⅓ cup / 85 g tahini

4 tablespoons / 60 ml fresh lemon juice

2 teaspoons honey or agave nectar

½ teaspoon sea salt

½ teaspoon freshly ground pepper

¼ cup / 60 ml extra-virgin olive oil

¼ cup / 60 ml water, as needed

Makes 1 cup / 240 ml

In a food processor or blender, blitz the garlic clove and serrano to mince. Add the herbs and blitz again. Add the miso paste, tahini, lemon juice, honey or agave, salt, pepper, and olive oil and pulse a few times to mix. With the motor running, add water, 1 tablespoon at a time, until you reach your desired thickness, noting it will firm up in the fridge. Season to taste.

This will keep covered in the fridge for a week or two.

Everyday Pesto

Salsa Mercado

Aji Verde

Romesco-ish

Green Harissa

Quick Pickled Onions

Double Mustard Maple Dressing

Avocado Pepita Sauce

Another Green Sauce

We have this around for grilled steaks, to put on a breakfast sandwich, to stir into any cooked grain, or to have with roasted vegetables or a pasta salad. Add half a can of white beans and now you have a dip for a crudité platter. Combined with a bit of mayo or butter for steamed artichoke dipping, or thinned with more lemon as a salad dressing, it's the bump of color and flavor every meal needs.

For more body, a quarter cup of salted pistachios are a great addition, added with the first pulse of things.

2 cloves garlic

2 slices of serrano pepper

1 teaspoon white or yellow miso paste

1 cup / 20 g flat-leaf parsley

1 cup / 20 g basil

¼ cup / 60 g chopped green onions
(or 3 slices of white part of a leek)

1 teaspoon sea salt

⅓ cup / 90 ml extra-virgin olive oil

2 teaspoons honey

1 tablespoon apple cider vinegar

2 tablespoons fresh lemon juice

Pinch of red pepper flakes

Makes ½ cup / 120 ml

In a food processor or blender, pulse the garlic, serrano, miso, parsley, basil, green onions or leeks, and salt until minced. Add the oil, honey, cider vinegar, lemon juice, and pinch of pepper flakes. Run until mostly smooth.

Transfer the sauce to a container and store in the fridge for up to a week.

Romesco-ish

This is always a favorite on the table for backyard BBQs. It's great with any grilled meat, roasted potatoes, or grilled asparagus, or as a spread on a veggie sandwich.

We usually buy the roasted peppers jarred. If you want to char them from scratch, start with about two medium bell peppers, char them over a hot grill or under a broiler until the skin blackens, let them rest, covered, then peel that blackened part off (doesn't have to be perfect), and proceed.

2 cloves garlic, chopped

½ cup / 57 g slivered almonds

1 (12-ounce / 340 g) jar roasted red peppers, drained

1 tablespoon lemon juice

2 tablespoons red wine vinegar

1 tablespoon honey

¼ cup / 60 g sundried tomatoes, in oil

1½ teaspoons smoked paprika

¼ teaspoon cayenne

1 teaspoon sea salt

Freshly ground pepper

Giant handful of fresh parsley

5 tablespoons / 75 ml extra-virgin olive oil
+ more for cooking

Makes 1 heaping cup / 240 ml

Heat a pan over medium heat with a thin slick of oil. Add the garlic and almonds and sauté for about 4 minutes until golden and fragrant. Set aside to cool.

In a blender or food processor, combine all the ingredients and pulse until mostly smooth; keep a bit of the texture. Adjust the seasoning to taste.

Store the sauce in the fridge for up to a week.

Gorgonzola Vinaigrette

I usually keep this one chunky, and spoon it over perfect summer tomatoes. My mom used to make an appetizer of this sort of dressing with a bunch of chopped tomatoes, parsley, and red onions that you'd spoon on top of toasted crostini. It goes on a grilled burger or some greens or grains. Consider a butter lettuce salad with fresh figs, toasted nuts, and some of this dressing.

I make it all in a bowl and keep it rustic, but it can be pulsed in a food processor or blender to get more of a salad dressing texture and smaller flecks of cheese.

2 tablespoons minced shallot

⅓ cup / 40 g crumbled gorgonzola

1 teaspoon Dijon mustard

½ teaspoon sea salt

¼ cup / 5 g chopped flat-leaf parsley

⅓ cup / 80 ml white wine vinegar

⅓ cup / 80 ml extra-virgin olive oil

Makes 1 cup / 240 ml

In a bowl, combine the shallot, gorgonzola, mustard, salt, parsley, and vinegar. Use the back of a fork to mash everything together to combine and get the cheese into smaller pieces. Begin to whisk, and slowly drizzle in the olive oil while whisking to create an emulsion. Alternatively, blitz the ingredients in a food processor and drizzle in the olive oil from there.

The dressing will keep stored in the fridge for a week.

Everything Cashew Sauce

Soak the cashews in water for at least an hour, up to overnight. We like this on Winter Bowls (page 191), as a dip with any roasted vegetable, for chicken tenders, a ramen noodle salad, or as part of a crudité platter.

Bragg's can be found at any well-stocked market. Coconut aminos work as a substitute. Almonds can be used in place of the cashews to mimic the popular store-bought dip Bitchin' Sauce.

¾ cup / 105 g raw cashews,
soaked in water for at least 1 hour

½ cup / 120 ml water

2 tablespoons avocado oil

1 tablespoon nutritional yeast

2 cloves garlic, chopped

2 tablespoons white balsamic vinegar

2 teaspoons Bragg's liquid aminos

¼ cup / 60 ml lemon juice

¼ teaspoon turmeric

½ teaspoon chili powder

½ teaspoon sea salt, to taste

Freshly ground pepper

Makes 1 cup / 240 ml

In a blender or food processor, combine the drained cashews and remaining ingredients. Blend until smooth. Adjust with more liquid to thin to your desired texture. Season to taste.

The sauce will store for 1 to 2 weeks, covered, in the fridge.

Avocado Pepita Sauce

The ingredients suggest this sauce goes with Latin American food, but it truly works anywhere you need some creaminess: with grilled skewers, on a burger, in a wrap, as a chip or veggie dip, as an excellent fish taco sauce, on any kind of taco really, or on a burrito bowl. Avocados are temperamental, so this is best eaten within a few days.

2 cloves garlic, roughly chopped

3 green onions, white and light green parts, chopped

1 jalapeño, semi-seeded, roughly chopped

1 bundle of cilantro, ends trimmed, roughly chopped

Handful of fresh parsley leaves, roughly chopped

3 tablespoons / 45 ml olive oil

¼ cup / 60 ml water

Juice of 2 limes (about ¼ cup / 60 ml)

2 large ripe avocados

⅓ cup / 40 g toasted, salted pumpkin seeds

1 teaspoon sea salt + more as needed

Makes 1½ cups / 360 ml

In a food processor, combine the garlic, green onions, and jalapeño and blitz a few times to mince. Add the cilantro, parsley, olive oil, water, and lime juice and pulse a few times to combine.

Add the flesh of the avocados, pepitas, and salt and pulse again until mostly smooth. Add water, 1 tablespoon at a time, to loosen the sauce, if needed. Taste for seasoning and adjust to your preference.

The sauce will store in an airtight container in the fridge for 3 to 5 days.

Coconut-Peanut Stir-Fry Bowl Sauce

A bowl is underwhelming without a sauce. I am conditioned to say that about most meals now, as everything around here gets an uptick with a sauce or dressing to finish things. Condiments and garnishes are important!

You can use almond or cashew butter, as I know peanuts are a common allergy. And tahini works too. It all makes sense with Asian-inspired dishes.

Juice of 2 limes

1 teaspoon fish sauce, optional

1 tablespoon rice vinegar

3 tablespoons / 45 ml toasted sesame oil

2 teaspoons tamari or low-sodium soy sauce

1–2 tablespoons grated fresh ginger

⅓ cup / 85 g smooth natural peanut butter

1 tablespoon agave nectar

1 clove garlic, chopped

1 small jalapeño, seeds partially removed, chopped

⅓ cup / 80 ml coconut milk, well shaken

Handful of cilantro

Salt and pepper

Makes 1 cup / 240 ml

Put all the ingredients in a blender or food processor and blend until smooth. We want it to be pourable, so add a tablespoon of water if needed. Taste for seasoning.

The sauce will keep covered in the fridge for up to 2 weeks.

Double Mustard Maple Dressing

All fall and winter, when many meals are root vegetables and warm spices, this dressing belongs everywhere. It can calm bitter greens or perk up roasted squash. We make a quick lunch salad of leftover roasted chicken, lentils, apples, arugula, pecans, and this dressing. It really does go with most anything.

2 teaspoons whole grain mustard

2 teaspoons Dijon mustard

1 clove garlic, grated

2 tablespoons minced shallot

1 tablespoon maple syrup

¼ cup / 60 ml champagne vinegar

1 tablespoon orange juice

3 tablespoons / 45 ml lemon juice
(about ½ a lemon)

Pinch of dried Italian herbs

½ cup / 120 ml extra-virgin olive oil

1 teaspoon sea salt

Freshly ground black pepper

Makes 1 cup / 240 ml

Combine all the dressing ingredients in a jar or blender. Shake or blend them up until combined. Store in an airtight container in the fridge for up to 1 week.

Note that the shallots and garlic will get more pungent over time.

Quick Pickled Onions

You'll have noticed a lot of Tex-Mex and seasonal bowl foods around here, and these pickled onions are always on hand for such meals. I have kept the list of spices short for these to be made easily with pantry staples. When I am fully stocked, I will add a few coriander or fennel seeds to the pickling liquid, but this is still a perfect condiment without them.

1 medium red onion, peeled and halved lengthwise

⅔ cup / 160 ml red wine vinegar

⅓ cup / 80 ml water

1 teaspoon sea salt

2 tablespoons sugar

Pinch of whole peppercorns

1 bay leaf

Makes about 2 cups / 475 ml

Slice the onion into thin half-moons. Pack them into a glass jar.

In a medium saucepan, warm the vinegar, water, salt, sugar, peppercorns, and bay leaf, and stir occasionally until the sugar dissolves, about 2 minutes. Take the pan off the heat to cool to room temperature.

Transfer the liquid to the jar to submerge the onions, adding another glug of vinegar if needed to cover. Cover and transfer to the fridge to chill completely.

Store them in the fridge for up to a month.

Salad Crunchies

Also known as tiny croutons. They're excellent as a soup topper or on top of roasted vegetables or a Caesar salad for a bit of texture. The point is that we don't want it to be difficult to eat or rip up the roof of your mouth, so I pulse the bread in a processor. In the right circumstance, a sprinkle of grated Parm on these straight out of the oven is lovely.

½ of a country loaf, torn

3 tablespoons / 45 ml extra-virgin olive oil

1 teaspoon dried Italian seasoning

1 teaspoon sea salt

½ teaspoon freshly ground pepper

Makes 2 cups / 112 g

Preheat the oven to 375°F / 190°C. Line a rimmed baking sheet with parchment.

Put the torn bread into a food processor and give it about 3 to 6 pulses to get small pieces. Drizzle on the oil, seasoning, salt, and pepper and give them another pulse or two until the bread is lightly coated. Transfer the crumbs to a rimmed baking sheet and bake for 9 minutes until golden, shaking the pan halfway through. They will crisp up as they cool.

Crunchies can be stored in an airtight container for up to 2 days.

To make regular croutons, instead of blitzing the bread in a food processor, just discard the tough ends and cut or rip the loaf into imperfect, 1-inch / 2.5 cm cubes. Preheat the oven to 400°F / 200°C. Toss the cubes in enough olive oil to lightly coat. Season with salt and pepper. Spread the croutons in an even layer on a rimmed baking sheet and roast for 10-ish minutes. Remove to cool and crisp. They will keep in a covered container for up to 3 days.

Corn Tortillas

I like the ease of making these in a stand mixer, but they can definitely be made by hand.

For a frico crust, we sprinkle a bit of cheese on top of the tortilla before it gets flipped, so it crisps into the dough for an extra special taco.

It is best to use the dough the day it is made.

2 tablespoons vegetable shortening or lard, room temperature

1¼ cups / 300 ml warm water

Zest of 1 lime

½ teaspoon sea salt

1½ cups / 175 g masa harina

Makes 12 tortillas

In a stand mixer with the paddle attachment, combine the shortening, warm water, lime zest, salt, and masa. Run the motor until smooth and combined, about 3 minutes. You want a texture slightly more tender than Play-Doh, so adjust either way with masa or water. Let the mixture rest for 10 minutes. The dough can be made a few hours in advance and kept covered at room temperature.

Heat a cast-iron skillet over medium heat.

Line a tortilla press with plastic wrap or parchment paper. Roll about 3 tablespoons' worth of dough into a ball. Use the press to flatten your tortillas to about ¼ inch / 65 mm thick. Cook the tortilla for 2 minutes per side until you see golden patches. If you do the cheese frico as mentioned in the headnote, add 1 more minute. Repeat with the remaining dough.

Keep the tortillas wrapped in a barely damp dish towel while you cook, and use them as soon as possible.

Leftover tortillas can be wrapped tightly and refrigerated for a few days or frozen for a few months.

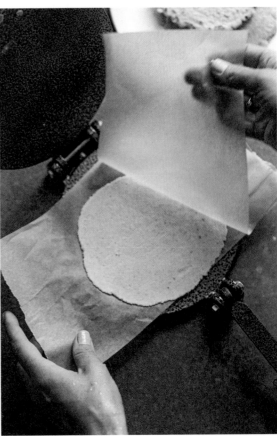

Day-Ahead Pizza Dough

I know, I'm asking you to plan ahead a day, but the hands-on time is simple. There are a few steps, but nothing is difficult, just worth a heads-up before you jump in. As it sits, the dough ferments, which is the element that adds flavor to a simple mixture of flour, water, and yeast. The only way to impart flavor into something as simple as plain pizza dough is time, so although this dough will still work if you use it within a few hours, it tastes better the next day and still works the day after that. The upside of that wait time is how quickly the dough comes together in the first place. Italian Tipo "00" flour and bread flours are available online, at Sprouts, or at Whole Foods and will yield an exceptional crust.

We save this for smaller family dinners or make a double batch when we fire up the backyard pizza oven for friends. The pizzas come out slowly, and everyone grazes throughout the process. This is the dough I use for Pizza Knots (page 74) and Butternut + Chorizo Flatbread (page 73) if I've planned ahead.

Scant ½ teaspoon active dry yeast

1–1¼ cups / 240–300 ml warm (not hot) water

2 teaspoons cane sugar

1½ cups / 180 g Tipo "00" flour or all-purpose flour

1½ cups / 180 g bread flour

1½ teaspoons sea salt

1 tablespoon extra-virgin olive oil + more for the bowl

Cornmeal or semolina

Makes dough for 2 or 3 small pizzas

Combine the yeast, 1 cup / 240 ml of the warm water, and the sugar in the bowl of a stand mixer, and let it sit a couple of minutes for the yeast to activate.

To the bowl of the stand mixer with a dough hook, add the flours and salt. Turn the mixer on low. Mix the dough for **3 minutes**, adding water if needed, 1 tablespoon at a time, to make a smooth ball. Scrape the dry flour down into the mix if you need to. Let it rest for **5 minutes**, add the oil, then mix it another **3 minutes**. The dough should look sticky but definitely resemble a loose ball and pull away from the sides. When you touch it, your hands will get sticky, but you should be able to transfer the ball.

Transfer the dough to an oiled bowl, cover it with plastic wrap, and keep it in the fridge for **at the very least 12 hours, ideally 24 hours, and up to 48 hours.** Don't even give it a second thought. It's just hanging out in there, needing zero attention.

On the day of pizza making, remove the dough from the refrigerator. Cover your work surface with a generous dusting of flour. Divide the dough into three parts, roll them through the flour and into balls, cover them with a dish towel, and let them proof at room temperature for 1 to 3 hours. The dough should increase in size, but rise time is weather and humidity dependent. If it's cold out, this will take longer.

When ready to cook, preheat your oven to 500°F / 260°C, along with a pizza stone, cast-iron skillet, or baking sheet. Prepare your toppings.

Use your hands to push and stretch the dough; use a light hand to keep some bubbles intact. If it tears, just patch it. Try not to touch the outer ½ inch / 1.25 cm.

Sprinkle cornmeal or semolina onto the hot stone/skillet/baking sheet and place your dough on top. Add sauce and toppings working quickly.

Bake the pizza in your very hot oven for about 8 minutes. Remove to cool slightly before slicing.

FAVORITE TOPPINGS
Butternut + Chorizo Flatbread (page 73)

Tomato sauce, mixed mozzarellas (fresh and low-moisture), pepper flakes + lemony arugula salad to top

Roasted fennel, red onion, olives + fontina

Roasted broccoli (chopped), pesto (page 280), fontina + Parm

Menu Ideas

We eat a lot of one-dish, bowl foods on weeknights, but when friends come over, I like to have more options. Below are a few menus that make sense together, most of which have make-ahead tips, so you don't feel stressed about pulling it all off.

Friends for a Summer BBQ

Smoky Eggplant Dip   58

Green Harissa Salmon Skewers with
Savory Peach + Cucumber Salad   141

Mixed Roasted Potatoes   131

Mixed Berry Crisp   252

Feeding a Group

Halloumi Skewers with Nectarines
+ Mint Chimichurri   77

Hawaiian Chicken Meatball Bowls   226

Sesame Cucumber Crunch   100

Aji Verde   282

Beachside Mai Tais   87

Cozy Night In

Day-Ahead Pizza Dough   292

Butternut + Chorizo Flatbread with
Pepita Pesto   73

Holiday Greens   126

Browned Butter Oatmeal
Chocolate Chip Cookies   251

A Family Birthday

Chicken Parmesan Meatballs   152

Arugula + Mapled Squash Salad   117

Birthday Cupcakes   268

Blackberry Gin Spritz   82

Baby/Bridal Shower

Pepper + Chorizo Breakfast Bake   42

Lemon Breakfast Loaf   34

Citrus Chicken Salad with
Goat Cheese Dressing   110

Watermelon Margaritas   85

Cherry Almond Bundt   257

Everyone Loves Tacos

Hugh's Guacamole 57

Taco Salad with Roasted Jalapeño
Ranch 175

Spicy Street Corn 132

Mushroom "Carnitas" 187

Quick Pickled Onions 289

Corn Tortillas 290

To Deliver to New Parents

Cinnamon-Apple Baked Oatmeal 24

Smoky Cauliflower Enchiladas 219

Anywhere Slaw 93

Chocolate-Covered Cashew
Cookie Dough Bites 244

Girls Night

Rosemary Nut + Pretzel Mix 64

Winter Bowls with Green Tahini 191

Honey Almond Fudge Bar 243

To Freeze for Your Future Self

Broccoli, Caramelized Onion
+ White Cheddar Quiche 27

Everyday Lentil Soup 198

Roasted Butternut Orzo Bake 217

Strawberry Rhubarb Crumble Bars 238

A Winter Holiday

Whipped Feta with Crushed Olives 61

Butternut Steaks with
Green Apple Relish 188

Mexican Caesar Brussels with
Cornbread Crispies 125

Gingersnap Pumpkin Tart 267

With Thanks

I am a little squeamish about writing this because I prefer to send these sorts of affirmations in personal notes, but these names absolutely bear mentioning to anyone who has enjoyed these pages, because I certainly didn't do it by myself.

Jenny Wapner and the team at Hardie Grant. This project felt like it took up a lot of runway in my life, waiting for the right person and publisher. Thank you for trusting me, Jenny, and for making the work better and more thoughtful with your expertise. You are an amazing editor, leader, and person, and I feel so lucky to have worked with you again.

The talented graphic designer, Ashley Lima, who kept pivoting along with us to get this book looking personal and usable. Katie Rumford for a proposal that kept me motivated for the final book through the toughest parts of this process. Andrianna deLone at CAA for helping get my book off the ground. Aran Goyoaga— thank you for all the ways you helped us with that last photoshoot in your beautiful space! You are endlessly talented and generous, and I am grateful for your support and friendship.

To my testers. Foremost, McKenzie Mitchell. McKenzie has worked for me for a few years, nearly since the birth of SK Cooking Club. I hired her (my first ever contractor!) because she was the most thorough and smart and honest and kind recipe tester I'd ever had in my career as a food writer. She is an incredible and humble cook, and has made so many of these recipes better, sometimes responsible for their genesis, and most importantly, she's been consistently encouraging of my work and all things Sprouted Kitchen. You are a treasure, Mack.

To Stacy Ladenburger, Sarah Kavlich, Nicole Marble, Katharyn Ridgeway, Jamie Finlayson, Erin Steed, Anne Killough, Larissa Wilson, and Mary Margaret Boudreaux. Your feedback was so imperative in making sure the food here makes sense. Thank you.

Hugh. I will tease but am absolutely serious that this SK stuff only happens because of you. Your imagery breathes warmth and beauty into this food. You are the conduit between my work and it being received and useful for others. Thank you for making everything so gorgeous, and for reminding me that I am creative and capable when I can't pump myself up to make any more food. You are my person, forever. I love you.

Curran and Cleo. No amount of book sales or Amazon reviews will ever matter as much to me as how you two see me. C + C, I tear up when I hear you tell someone that I am the "best cook" or when you ask me to make food to deliver to your teachers. Your secretly scribbled "I love you mommy" on all my recipe notepads in the kitchen made me smile every time I got working and found one. I hope you always want me to make you food and invite your friends to our house for meals. The title of this book is a tribute to you both—my favorite place.

Friends who picked up my kids from school or acted as free models when I told you I would cook you dinner but to please have clean nails for photos. My family, who constantly cheerleads my projects.

To all of you who have read the blog or are SK Cooking Club subscribers or bought our previous cookbooks or e-books or this one! I never imagined that this would be my career, but I feel so lucky to spend time making food and sharing recipes. This really is a dream job, and I am indescribably grateful for your support.

Index

A

Ahi Salad Bowls, Sesame Seared, 142
Aji Verde, 282
almonds
    Almond Flour Double Chocolate Cookies, 248
    Cherry Almond Bundt, 257
    Cleo's Morning Glory Oats, 39
    Granola Number 3, 31
    Holiday Greens, 126
    Honey Almond Fudge Bar, 243
    Mixed Berry Crisp, 252
    Quinoa Salad with Watermelon + Golden Beets, 99
    Romesco-ish, 286
    Strawberry Rhubarb Crumble Bars, 238–41
Aloha Greens, 47
apples
    Butternut Steaks with Green Apple Relish, 188–90
    Chopped Greens with Sweet Potatoes, Dates, Apples + Crispy Shallots, 104–5
    Cinnamon-Apple Baked Oatmeal, 24
    Feel-Good Green Smoothie, 47
    Harvest Breakfast Cake, 32
artichokes
    Summer Tortellini Salad, 232
arugula
    Arugula + Mapled Squash Salad, 117
    Butternut Steaks with Green Apple Relish, 188–90
    Chicken Milanese with Asparagus + Gribiche Salad, 148–51
    Chopped Greens with Sweet Potatoes, Dates, Apples + Crispy Shallots, 104–5

Citrus Chicken Salad with Goat Cheese Dressing, 110–12
Grilled Peach + Burrata Salad with Breadcrumb Crispies, 78
Lemon and Parm Broccoli, 121
Peach + Lentil Salad with Black Pepper Vinaigrette, 95
Quinoa Salad with Watermelon + Golden Beets, 99
Summer Tortellini Salad, 232
Tahini-Glazed Cauliflower, 122
asparagus
    Chicken Milanese with Asparagus + Gribiche Salad, 148–51
    Spring Spaghetti with Asparagus + Peas, 168
avocados
    Avocado Crema, 181
    Avocado Pepita Sauce, 288
    Avocado Toast with Crispy Za'atar Chickpeas, 15
    Blackened Salmon with Tropical Pico, 138
    Breakfast Salad, 20
    Citrus Chicken Salad with Goat Cheese Dressing, 110–12
    Hugh's Guacamole, 57
    Pepper + Chorizo Breakfast Bake, 43
    Sesame Cucumber Crunch, 100
    Sesame Noodle Slaw, 113–15
    Sesame Seared Ahi Salad Bowls, 142
    Taco Salad with Roasted Jalapeño Ranch, 175–76

B

bananas
    After-School Banana Chocolate Chip Chunkers, 81
    Aloha Greens, 47
    Banana Blender Pancakes, 16
    Berry Breakfast Smoothie, 47
    Chocolate Dreams, 47
    Pep-Start Shake, 47
bars
    Honey Almond Fudge Bar, 243
    Strawberry Rhubarb Crumble Bars, 238–41
basil
    Another Green Sauce, 286
    Everyday Pesto, 280
Beachside Mai Tais, 87
beans
    Italian Farro Soup, 201
    Smoky Cauliflower Enchiladas, 219–20
    Sweet Potato Taco Stew, 208
    Taco Salad with Roasted Jalapeño Ranch, 175–76
    Turkey Chili, 202
    The Veggie Burger with Roasted Tomatoes + Quick Pickles, 171–72
    White Bean Bruschetta, 70
    See also chickpeas; edamame
beef
    Mixed Mushroom Bolognese, 223
beets
    Beet Dip, 54
    Quinoa Salad with Watermelon + Golden Beets, 99
bell peppers
    Pepper + Chorizo Breakfast Bake, 43
    Romesco-ish, 286
berries
    Berry Breakfast Smoothie, 47
    Curran's Cocoa Berry Oats, 38

Mapled Berries, 17
Mixed Berry Crisp, 252
See also individual berries
Birthday Cupcakes, 268–69
Blackberry Gin Spritz, 82
bread
 Avocado Toast with Crispy
  Za'atar Chickpeas, 15
 Breakfast Salad, 20
 Butternut + Chorizo Flatbread
  with Pepita Pesto, 73
 Fattoush with Za'atar
  Lavash, 92
 French Bread Pizzas, 165
 Grilled Peach + Burrata
  Salad with Breadcrumb
  Crispies, 78
 Mexican Caesar Brussels with
  Cornbread Crispies, 125
 Salad Crunchies, 290
 Summer Panzanella Salad, 96
 White Bean Bruschetta, 70
Breakfast Salad, 20
broccoli
 Broccoli, Caramelized
  Onion + White Cheddar
  Quiche, 27–28
 Lemon and Parm Broccoli, 121
Brownies, Peppermint, with
 Ganache, 271–72
Bruschetta, White Bean, 70
Brussels sprouts
 Holiday Greens, 126
 Mexican Caesar Brussels with
  Cornbread Crispies, 125
Budinos, Dairy-Free Chocolate
 Peanut Butter, 277
burgers
 Italian Turkey Burgers with
  Frico Crisps, 158–61
 The Veggie Burger with
  Roasted Tomatoes +
  Quick Pickles, 171–72
butternut squash
 Arugula + Mapled Squash
  Salad, 117
 Butternut + Chorizo Flatbread
  with Pepita Pesto, 73
 Butternut Steaks with Green
  Apple Relish, 188–90
 Gingered Butternut Soup, 211

Roasted Butternut Orzo Bake,
 217–18
Turkey Chili, 202

C
cabbage
 Anywhere Slaw, 93
 Curried Carrot Salad, 103
 Hawaiian Chicken Meatball
  Bowls, 226–27
 Sesame Cucumber Crunch, 100
 Sesame Noodle Slaw, 113–15
 Sloppy Jane Sweet Potato
  Boats, 229–30
 Sweet Potato Taco Stew, 208
 Taco Salad with Roasted
  Jalapeño Ranch, 175–76
cakes
 Birthday Cupcakes, 268–69
 Cherry Almond Bundt, 257
 Harvest Breakfast Cake, 32
 Lemon Breakfast Loaf, 34
 Memaw's Peach Cake, 258
 Our One-Bowl Carrot
  Cake, 263–64
Caramel, Vegan Coconut, 247
carrots
 Carrot + Red Lentil Dal, 207
 Curried Carrot Salad, 103
 Jeweled Farro Salad with
  Caramelized Carrots +
  Pomegranate Seeds, 118
 Our One-Bowl Carrot
  Cake, 263–64
cashews
 Cauliflower Tikka Masala, 212
 Chocolate-Covered Cashew
  Cookie Dough Bites, 244
 Curried Carrot Salad, 103
 Everything Cashew
  Sauce, 287–88
 Rosemary Nut + Pretzel
  Mix, 64
 Tofu + Mushroom Lettuce
  Wraps, 178
cauliflower
 Cauliflower Al Pastor
  Bowls, 181
 Cauliflower Tikka Masala, 212
 Curried Chickpea Bowls, 203
 Feel-Good Green Smoothie, 47

Pasta with Roasted
 Cauliflower, Chorizo +
 Winter Pesto, 173
Smoky Cauliflower
 Enchiladas, 219–20
Tahini-Glazed Cauliflower, 122
Winter Bowls with Green
 Tahini, 191–93
chard
 Chicken Parmesan Meatballs,
  152–55
 Italian Farro Soup, 201
 Jeweled Farro Salad with
  Caramelized Carrots +
  Pomegranate Seeds, 118
cheese
 Broccoli, Caramelized
  Onion + White Cheddar
  Quiche, 27–28
 Chicken Parmesan
  Meatballs, 152–55
 French Bread Pizzas, 165
 Goat Cheese Dressing, 110
 Gorgonzola Vinaigrette, 287
 Grilled Peach + Burrata
  Salad with Breadcrumb
  Crispies, 78
 Halloumi Skewers with
  Nectarines + Mint
  Chimichurri, 77
 Italian Turkey Burgers with
  Frico Crisps, 158–61
 Lemon and Parm Broccoli, 121
 Mushroom Quesadillas with
  Sunflower Seed Crema, 69
 Roasted Eggplant Rollups, 182
 Smoky Cauliflower
  Enchiladas, 219–20
 Whipped Feta with Crushed
  Olives, 61
Cherry Almond Bundt, 257
chia seeds
 Berry Breakfast Smoothie, 47
 Curran's Cocoa Berry Oats, 38
chicken
 Chicken Milanese with
  Asparagus + Gribiche
  Salad, 148–51
 Chicken Parmesan
  Meatballs, 152–55

Citrus Chicken Salad
with Goat Cheese Dressing,
110–12
Corn Chip Chicken Nuggets
with Yogurt Ranch, 233–35
Curried Chickpea Bowls, 203
Fattoush with Za'atar
Lavash, 92
Hawaiian Chicken Meatball
Bowls, 226–27
Sweet Potato Taco Stew, 208
There's Always Chicken, 157
chickpeas
Avocado Toast with Crispy
Za'atar Chickpeas, 15
Curried Carrot Salad, 103
Curried Chickpea Bowls, 203
Summer Tortellini Salad, 232
chiles
Aji Verde, 282
Green Harissa, 281
Roasted Jalapeño Ranch, 175
Salsa Mercado, 282
Smoky Cauliflower
Enchiladas, 219–20
Chili, Turkey, 202
Chimichurri, Mint, 77
chocolate
After-School Banana
Chocolate Chip
Chunkers, 81
Almond Flour Double
Chocolate Cookies, 248
Birthday Cupcakes, 268–69
Browned Butter Oatmeal
Chocolate Chip
Cookies, 251
Chocolate-Covered Cashew
Cookie Dough Bites, 244
Chocolate Dreams, 47
Chocolate Ganache, 272
Dairy-Free Chocolate Peanut
Butter Budinos, 277
Honey Almond Fudge Bar, 243
Peppermint Brownies with
Ganache, 271–72
chorizo. See sausage
cinnamon
Cinnamon-Apple Baked
Oatmeal, 24
Sweet Potato Cinnamon Rolls,
48–49

Cleo's Morning Glory Oats, 39
coconut
Cauliflower Tikka Masala, 212
Cleo's Morning Glory Oats, 39
Curried Carrot Salad, 103
Granola Number 3, 31
Harvest Breakfast Cake, 32
Mixed Berry Crisp, 252
Our One-Bowl Carrot
Cake, 263–64
Sesame Noodle Slaw, 113–15
coconut cream
Curried Chickpea Bowls, 203
Everyday Lentil Soup, 198
Vegan Coconut Caramel, 247
coconut milk
Aloha Greens, 47
Carrot + Red Lentil Dal, 207
Coconut-Peanut Stir-Fry
Bowl Sauce, 288–89
Coconut Rice, 138, 142,
226–27
Dairy-Free Chocolate Peanut
Butter Budinos, 277
Everyday Lentil Soup, 198
Gingered Butternut Soup, 211
Hawaiian Chicken Meatball
Bowls, 226–27
Pep-Start Shake, 47
coffee
Pep-Start Shake, 47
Cointreau
Beachside Mai Tais, 87
conversations, starting, 109
cookies
Almond Flour Double
Chocolate Cookies, 248
Browned Butter Oatmeal
Chocolate Chip
Cookies, 251
corn
Corn Chip Chicken Nuggets
with Yogurt Ranch, 233–35
Corn Tortillas, 290–91
A Crispy Cornmeal Waffle, 12
Spicy Street Corn, 132
Sweet Potato Taco Stew, 208
Taco Salad with Roasted
Jalapeño Ranch, 175–76
Couscous, Harissa Lamb
Meatballs with, 163–64

crema
Avocado Crema, 181
Sunflower Seed Crema, 69
Crisp, Mixed Berry, 252
cucumbers
Green Harissa Salmon
Skewers with Savory Peach
+ Cucumber Salad, 141
Quick Pickles, 171
Sesame Cucumber
Crunch, 100
Cupcakes, Birthday, 268–69
Curran's Cocoa Berry Oats, 38

D
Dal, Carrot + Red Lentil, 207
dates
Chocolate-Covered Cashew
Cookie Dough Bites, 244
Chopped Greens with Sweet
Potatoes, Dates, Apples +
Crispy Shallots, 104–5
Shallot Date Vinaigrette, 283
Tahini-Glazed
Cauliflower, 122
delicata squash
Arugula + Mapled Squash
Salad, 117
dips
Beet Dip, 54
Hugh's Guacamole, 57
Smoky Eggplant Dip, 58
drinks
Beachside Mai Tais, 87
Blackberry Gin Spritz, 82
Watermelon Margaritas, 85

E
edamame
Sesame Cucumber Crunch, 100
eggplant
Roasted Eggplant Rollups, 182
Smoky Eggplant Dip, 58
eggs
Breakfast Salad, 20
Broccoli, Caramelized
Onion + White Cheddar
Quiche, 27–28
Pepper + Chorizo Breakfast
Bake, 43

enchiladas
    Enchilada Sauce, 219
    Smoky Cauliflower
      Enchiladas, 219–20
equipment, 6–7

F

farro
    Italian Farro Soup, 201
    Jeweled Farro Salad with
      Caramelized Carrots +
      Pomegranate Seeds, 118
Fattoush with Za'atar Lavash, 92
Feel-Good Green Smoothie, 47
fish
    Blackened Salmon with
      Tropical Pico, 138
    Sesame Seared Ahi Salad
      Bowls, 142
French Bread Pizzas, 165

G

Ganache, Chocolate, 272
Gingered Butternut Soup, 211
Gingersnap Pumpkin Tart, 267
Gin Spritz, Blackberry, 82
Granola Number 3, 31
grapefruit
    Blackberry Gin Spritz, 82
    Citrus Chicken Salad with
      Goat Cheese Dressing,
      110–12
greens
    Aloha Greens, 47
    Chopped Greens with Sweet
      Potatoes, Dates, Apples +
      Crispy Shallots, 104–5
    Holiday Greens, 126
    Winter Bowls with Green
      Tahini, 191–93
    See also individual greens
Guacamole, Hugh's, 57

H

ham
    French Bread Pizzas, 165
harissa
    Green Harissa, 281
    Green Harissa Salmon
      Skewers with Savory Peach
      + Cucumber Salad, 141

Harissa Lamb Meatballs with
    Couscous, 163–64
Harvest Breakfast Cake, 32
Hawaiian Chicken Meatball
    Bowls, 226–27
hemp seeds
    Berry Breakfast Smoothie, 47
    Breakfast Salad, 20
    Feel-Good Green Smoothie, 47
    Pep-Start Shake, 47
Holiday Greens, 126
honey
    Honey Almond Fudge Bar, 243
    Honey Miso Dressing, 100
Hugh's Guacamole, 57

I

Italian Farro Soup, 201
Italian Turkey Burgers with
    Frico Crisps, 158–61

J

Jeweled Farro Salad with
    Caramelized Carrots +
    Pomegranate Seeds, 118

K

kale
    Anywhere Slaw, 93
    Breakfast Salad, 20
    Chopped Greens with Sweet
      Potatoes, Dates, Apples +
      Crispy Shallots, 104–5
    Citrus Chicken Salad with
      Goat Cheese Dressing,
      110–12
    Everyday Lentil Soup, 198
    Feel-Good Green Smoothie, 47
    Hawaiian Chicken Meatball
      Bowls, 226–27
    Holiday Greens, 126
    Italian Farro Soup, 201
    Jeweled Farro Salad with
      Caramelized Carrots +
      Pomegranate Seeds, 118
    Kale Pesto, 173
    Pepper + Chorizo Breakfast
      Bake, 43
    Roasted Butternut Orzo
      Bake, 217–18
Key Lime Pie, 254

L

Lamb Meatballs, Harissa,
    with Couscous, 163–64
lemons
    Blackberry Gin Spritz, 82
    Citrus Chicken Salad with
      Goat Cheese Dressing,
      110–12
    Lemon and Parm Broccoli, 121
    Lemon Breakfast Loaf, 34
lentils
    Carrot + Red Lentil Dal, 207
    Chopped Greens with Sweet
      Potatoes, Dates, Apples +
      Crispy Shallots, 104–5
    Everyday Lentil Soup, 198
    Mixed Mushroom
      Bolognese, 223
    Peach + Lentil Salad with
      Black Pepper Vinaigrette, 95
lettuce
    Chopped Greens with Sweet
      Potatoes, Dates, Apples +
      Crispy Shallots, 104–5
    Fattoush with Za'atar
      Lavash, 92
    Peach + Lentil Salad with
      Black Pepper Vinaigrette, 95
    Tofu + Mushroom Lettuce
      Wraps, 178
limes
    Anywhere Slaw, 93
    Beachside Mai Tais, 87
    Key Lime Pie, 254
    Watermelon Margaritas, 85

M

Mai Tais, Beachside, 87
mangoes
    Aloha Greens, 47
    Tropical Pico, 62
maple syrup
    Arugula + Mapled Squash
      Salad, 117
    Double Mustard Maple
      Dressing, 289
    Mapled Berries, 17
Margaritas, Watermelon, 85
meatballs
    Chicken Parmesan
      Meatballs, 152–55

Harissa Lamb Meatballs with
Couscous, 163–64
Hawaiian Chicken Meatball
Bowls, 226–27
Memaw's Peach Cake, 258
menu ideas, 294–95
Mexican Caesar, 280–81
Mexican Caesar Brussels with
Cornbread Crispies, 125
Mint Chimichurri, 77
Miso Dressing, Honey, 100
Muffins, Pumpkin, with Pepita
Crumble, 44
mushrooms
Mixed Mushroom
Bolognese, 223
Mushroom "Carnitas," 187
Mushroom Quesadillas with
Sunflower Seed Crema, 69
Tofu + Mushroom Lettuce
Wraps, 178
Mustard Maple Dressing,
Double, 289

N
Nectarines, Halloumi Skewers
with, 77
noodles. *See* pasta and noodles
nuts
Cleo's Morning Glory Oats, 39
Granola Number 3, 31
Rosemary Nut + Pretzel
Mix, 64
See also individual nuts

O
oats
After-School Banana
Chocolate Chip
Chunkers, 81
Banana Blender Pancakes, 16
Berry Breakfast Smoothie, 47
Browned Butter Oatmeal
Chocolate Chip Cookies, 251
Cinnamon-Apple Baked
Oatmeal, 24
Cleo's Morning Glory Oats, 39
Curran's Cocoa Berry Oats, 38
Gingersnap Pumpkin Tart, 267
Granola Number 3, 31
Mixed Berry Crisp, 252

Pumpkin Muffins with Pepita
Crumble, 44
Strawberry Rhubarb Crumble
Bars, 238–41
The Veggie Burger with
Roasted Tomatoes + Quick
Pickles, 171–72
olives
Summer Tortellini Salad, 232
Whipped Feta with Crushed
Olives, 61
onions
Broccoli, Caramelized Onion
+ White Cheddar Quiche,
27–28
Quick Pickled Onions, 289
oranges
Beachside Mai Tais, 87
Citrus Chicken Salad with
Goat Cheese Dressing,
110–12

P
Pancakes, Banana Blender, 16
Panzanella Salad, Summer, 96
pasta and noodles
Mixed Mushroom
Bolognese, 223
Pasta with Roasted
Cauliflower, Chorizo
+ Winter Pesto, 173
Roasted Butternut Orzo
Bake, 217–18
Sesame Noodle Slaw, 113–15
Spring Spaghetti with
Asparagus + Peas, 168
Summer Tortellini Salad, 232
peaches
Green Harissa Salmon
Skewers with Savory Peach
+ Cucumber Salad, 141
Grilled Peach + Burrata
Salad with Breadcrumb
Crispies, 78
Memaw's Peach Cake, 258
Peach + Lentil Salad with
Black Pepper Vinaigrette, 95
Summer Panzanella Salad, 96
peanuts and peanut butter
Coconut-Peanut Stir-Fry Bowl
Sauce, 288–89

Dairy-Free Chocolate Peanut
Butter Budinos, 277
Honey Miso Dressing, 100
pears
Feel-Good Green Smoothie, 47
Gingered Butternut Soup, 211
peas
Sesame Cucumber Crunch, 100
Spring Spaghetti with
Asparagus + Peas, 168
pecans
Cinnamon-Apple Baked
Oatmeal, 24
Cleo's Morning Glory Oats, 39
Rosemary Nut + Pretzel
Mix, 64
Sweet Potato Cinnamon
Rolls, 48–49
pepitas (pumpkin seeds)
Anywhere Slaw, 93
Arugula + Mapled Squash
Salad, 117
Avocado Pepita Sauce, 288
Cauliflower Al Pastor
Bowls, 181
Feel-Good Green Smoothie, 47
Granola Number 3, 31
Mexican Caesar Brussels with
Cornbread Crispies, 125
Peach + Lentil Salad with
Black Pepper Vinaigrette, 95
Pepita Pesto, 73
Pumpkin Muffins with Pepita
Crumble, 44
Sloppy Jane Sweet Potato
Boats, 229–30
Taco Salad with Roasted
Jalapeño Ranch, 175–76
Peppermint Brownies with
Ganache, 271–72
Pep-Start Shake, 47
pesto
Everyday Pesto, 280
Kale Pesto, 173
Pepita Pesto, 73
Pico, Tropical, 62
Pie, Key Lime, 254
pineapple
Aloha Greens, 47
Beachside Mai Tais, 87

Cauliflower Al Pastor
Bowls, 181
Hawaiian Chicken Meatball
Bowls, 226–27
Kale Pesto, 173
Our One-Bowl Carrot
Cake, 263–64
Shrimp + Pineapple Sheet Pan
Tacos, 147
Tropical Pico, 62
pine nuts
Chicken Milanese with
Asparagus + Gribiche
Salad, 148–51
Everyday Pesto, 280
Grilled Peach + Burrata
Salad with Breadcrumb
Crispies, 78
Kale Pesto, 173
Lemon and Parm Broccoli, 121
Roasted Eggplant Rollups, 182
Summer Tortellini Salad, 232
Tahini-Glazed Cauliflower, 122
Whipped Feta with Crushed
Olives, 61
pistachios
Citrus Chicken Salad with
Goat Cheese Dressing,
110–12
Jeweled Farro Salad with
Caramelized Carrots +
Pomegranate Seeds, 118
Roasted Butternut Orzo Bake,
217–18
Spring Spaghetti with
Asparagus + Peas, 168
Winter Bowls with Green
Tahini, 191–93
pizza
Day-Ahead Pizza
Dough, 292–93
French Bread Pizzas, 165
Pizza Knots, 74
polenta
Chicken Parmesan
Meatballs, 152–55
Mixed Mushroom
Bolognese, 223
pomegranates
Holiday Greens, 126

Jeweled Farro Salad with
Caramelized Carrots +
Pomegranate Seeds, 118
potatoes
Broccoli, Caramelized
Onion + White Cheddar
Quiche, 27–28
Curried Chickpea Bowls, 203
Mixed Roasted Potatoes, 131
Winter Bowls with Green
Tahini, 191–93
pretzels
Rosemary Nut + Pretzel
Mix, 64
prosciutto
French Bread Pizzas, 165
pumpkin
Gingersnap Pumpkin Tart, 267
Pumpkin Muffins with Pepita
Crumble, 44
See also pepitas

Q

Quesadillas, Mushroom, with
Sunflower Seed Crema, 69
questions for the dinner table, 109
Quiche, Broccoli, Caramelized
Onion + White Cheddar,
27–28
quinoa
Butternut Steaks with Green
Apple Relish, 188–90
Peach + Lentil Salad with
Black Pepper Vinaigrette, 95
Quinoa Salad with
Watermelon + Golden
Beets, 99
Winter Bowls with Green
Tahini, 191–93

R

raisins
Cleo's Morning Glory Oats, 39
Curried Carrot Salad, 103
Jeweled Farro Salad with
Caramelized Carrots +
Pomegranate Seeds, 118
Rhubarb Crumble Bars,
Strawberry, 238–41

rice
Blackened Salmon with
Tropical Pico, 138
Carrot + Red Lentil Dal, 207
Cauliflower Al Pastor
Bowls, 181
Cauliflower Tikka Masala, 212
Coconut Rice, 138, 142,
226–27
Curried Chickpea Bowls, 203
Hawaiian Chicken Meatball
Bowls, 226–27
Sesame Seared Ahi Salad
Bowls, 142
The Veggie Burger with
Roasted Tomatoes + Quick
Pickles, 171–72
Rolls, Sweet Potato Cinnamon,
48–49
Romesco-ish, 286
Rosemary Nut + Pretzel Mix, 64
rum
Beachside Mai Tais, 87

S

salad dressings
Double Mustard Maple
Dressing, 289
Goat Cheese Dressing, 110
Honey Miso Dressing, 100
Mexican Caesar, 280–81
Roasted Jalapeño Ranch, 175
Yogurt Ranch, 235
See also vinaigrettes
salads
Arugula + Mapled Squash
Salad, 117
Asparagus + Gribiche Salad,
148–51
Breakfast Salad, 20
Chopped Greens with Sweet
Potatoes, Dates, Apples +
Crispy Shallots, 104–5
Citrus Chicken Salad with
Goat Cheese Dressing,
110–12
Curried Carrot Salad, 103
Fattoush with Za'atar
Lavash, 92

Grilled Peach + Burrata
Salad with Breadcrumb
Crispies, 78
Jeweled Farro Salad with
Caramelized Carrots +
Pomegranate Seeds, 118
Peach + Lentil Salad with
Black Pepper Vinaigrette, 95
Quinoa Salad with
Watermelon + Golden
Beets, 99
Salad Crunchies, 290
Savory Peach + Cucumber
Salad, 141
Sesame Cucumber Crunch, 100
Sesame Seared Ahi Salad
Bowls, 142
Summer Panzanella Salad, 96
Summer Tortellini Salad, 232
Taco Salad with Roasted
Jalapeño Ranch, 175–76
See also slaws
salami
Summer Tortellini Salad, 232
salmon
Blackened Salmon with
Tropical Pico, 138
Green Harissa Salmon
Skewers with Savory Peach
+ Cucumber Salad, 141
sauces and salsas
Aji Verde, 282
Another Green Sauce, 286
Avocado Pepita Sauce, 288
Coconut-Peanut Stir-Fry Bowl
Sauce, 288–89
Enchilada Sauce, 219
Everything Cashew Sauce,
287–88
Mint Chimichurri, 77
Mixed Mushroom
Bolognese, 223
Romesco-ish, 286
Salsa Mercado, 282
Tropical Pico, 62
See also pesto
sausage
Butternut + Chorizo Flatbread
with Pepita Pesto, 73
Italian Farro Soup, 201

Pasta with Roasted
Cauliflower, Chorizo +
Winter Pesto, 173
Pepper + Chorizo Breakfast
Bake, 43
seeds
Cleo's Morning Glory Oats, 39
Granola Number 3, 31
See also individual seeds
sesame seeds
Hawaiian Chicken Meatball
Bowls, 226–27
Sesame Cucumber Crunch, 100
Sesame Noodle Slaw, 113–15
Sesame Seared Ahi Salad
Bowls, 142
Smoky Eggplant Dip, 58
Tahini-Glazed
Cauliflower, 122
See also tahini
Shallot Date Vinaigrette, 283
Shrimp + Pineapple Sheet Pan
Tacos, 147
skewers
Green Harissa Salmon
Skewers with Savory Peach
+ Cucumber Salad, 141
Halloumi Skewers with
Nectarines + Mint
Chimichurri, 77
slaws
Anywhere Slaw, 93
Sesame Noodle Slaw, 113–15
Sloppy Jane Sweet Potato
Boats, 229–30
smoothies
Aloha Greens, 47
Berry Breakfast Smoothie, 47
Chocolate Dreams, 47
Feel-Good Green Smoothie, 47
making, 46
Pep-Start Shake, 47
soups
Everyday Lentil Soup, 198
Gingered Butternut Soup, 211
Italian Farro Soup, 201
spinach
Aloha Greens, 47
Carrot + Red Lentil Dal, 207
Chocolate Dreams, 47

Pepper + Chorizo Breakfast
Bake, 43
Spring Spaghetti with Asparagus
+ Peas, 168
squash. See butternut squash;
delicata squash; zucchini
strawberries
A Crispy Cornmeal Waffle, 12
Mixed Berry Crisp, 252
Strawberry Rhubarb Crumble
Bars, 238–41
Summer Panzanella Salad, 96
Summer Tortellini Salad, 232
sunflower seeds
Cleo's Morning Glory Oats, 39
Mushroom Quesadillas with
Sunflower Seed Crema, 69
sweet potatoes
Chopped Greens with Sweet
Potatoes, Dates, Apples +
Crispy Shallots, 104–5
Everyday Lentil Soup, 198
Mixed Roasted Potatoes, 131
Mushroom Quesadillas with
Sunflower Seed Crema, 69
Pepper + Chorizo Breakfast
Bake, 43
Sloppy Jane Sweet Potato
Boats, 229–30
Sweet Potato Cinnamon Rolls,
48–49
Sweet Potato Taco Stew, 208
Taco Salad with Roasted
Jalapeño Ranch, 175–76
The Veggie Burger with
Roasted Tomatoes + Quick
Pickles, 171–72

T
Tacos, Shrimp + Pineapple Sheet
Pan, 147
Taco Salad with Roasted
Jalapeño Ranch, 175–76
Taco Stew, Sweet Potato, 208
tahini
Avocado Toast with Crispy
Za'atar Chickpeas, 15
Green Tahini, 283
Honey Miso Dressing, 100
Sesame Noodle Slaw, 113–15
Smoky Eggplant Dip, 58

Tahini-Glazed
  Cauliflower, 122
Tart, Gingersnap Pumpkin, 267
tequila
  Watermelon Margaritas, 85
The Veggie Burger with Roasted
  Tomatoes + Quick Pickles,
  171–72
Tikka Masala, Cauliflower, 212
tofu
  Sesame Noodle Slaw, 113–15
  Tofu + Mushroom Lettuce
    Wraps, 178
  Winter Bowls with Green
    Tahini, 191–93
tomatoes
  Avocado Toast with Crispy
    Za'atar Chickpeas, 15
  Breakfast Salad, 20
  Curried Chickpea Bowls, 203
  Everyday Lentil Soup, 198
  Fattoush with Za'atar
    Lavash, 92
  Grilled Peach + Burrata
    Salad with Breadcrumb
    Crispies, 78
  Harissa Lamb Meatballs with
    Couscous, 163–64
  Italian Farro Soup, 201
  Mixed Mushroom
    Bolognese, 223
  Pepper + Chorizo Breakfast
    Bake, 43
  Pizza Knots, 74
  Romesco-ish, 286
  Salsa Mercado, 282
  Sloppy Jane Sweet Potato
    Boats, 229–30
  Summer Panzanella Salad, 96
  Summer Tortellini Salad, 232
  Sweet Potato Taco Stew, 208
  Tropical Pico, 62
  Turkey Chili, 202
  The Veggie Burger with
    Roasted Tomatoes + Quick
    Pickles, 171–72
  Whipped Feta with Crushed
    Olives, 61
  White Bean Bruschetta, 70
tortillas
  Corn Tortillas, 290–91

Mushroom Quesadillas with
  Sunflower Seed Crema, 69
Shrimp + Pineapple Sheet Pan
  Tacos, 147
Smoky Cauliflower
  Enchiladas, 219–20
Tropical Pico, 62
turkey
  Italian Turkey Burgers with
    Frico Crisps, 158–61
  Mixed Mushroom
    Bolognese, 223
  Sloppy Jane Sweet Potato
    Boats, 229–30
  Turkey Chili, 202

V
vinaigrettes
  Black Pepper Vinaigrette, 95
  Gorgonzola Vinaigrette, 287
  Shallot Date Vinaigrette, 283

W
Waffle, A Crispy Cornmeal, 12
walnuts
  Beet Dip, 54
  Harvest Breakfast Cake, 32
  Our One-Bowl Carrot
    Cake, 263–64
  Rosemary Nut + Pretzel
    Mix, 64
  The Veggie Burger with
    Roasted Tomatoes + Quick
    Pickles, 171–72
watermelon
  Quinoa Salad with
    Watermelon + Golden
    Beets, 99
  Watermelon Margaritas, 85
Winter Bowls with Green
  Tahini, 191–93

Y
Yogurt Ranch, 235

Z
zucchini
  Harvest Breakfast Cake, 32
  Roasted Eggplant Rollups,
    182

About the Author

Sara Forte has been writing and sharing vegetable-forward, practical recipes by way of her food blog, Instagram, and meal-planning program since 2010. Her first cookbook title, *The Sprouted Kitchen*, was a James Beard–nominated cookbook in 2012, followed by *Sprouted Kitchen Bowl + Spoon* in 2015. Her recipes have been featured in *Oprah*, *Sunset*, *Rachel Ray*, *Better Homes and Gardens*, and *The Today Show*, among other publications. Her career the past few years has been dedicated to making dinnertime more efficient and delicious by providing weekly plans by way of her Cooking Club.

Sara and her husband, Hugh, live in Southern California with their kids, Curran and Cleo, and spend free time at the beach, searching for the perfect local tacos, and sharing citrusy tequila cocktails with friends at their home.